The Outperformers

Lessons from Top Law Firm Leaders

Authors
Kent Zimmermann, Patrick Smith and Carlyn Kolker

Managing director
Sian O'Neill

The Outperformers: Lessons from Top Law Firm Leaders
is published by

Globe Law and Business Ltd
3 Mylor Close
Horsell
Woking
Surrey GU21 4DD
United Kingdom
Tel: +44 20 3745 4770
www.globelawandbusiness.com

Printed and bound by 4Edge Ltd, Hockley, Essex

The Outperformers: Lessons from Top Law Firm Leaders

ISBN 9781837231034
EPUB ISBN 9781837231041
Adobe PDF 9781837231058

About Globe Law and Business

Globe Law and Business was established in 2005. From the very beginning, we set out to create legal books that are sufficiently high level to be of real use to the experienced professional, yet still accessible and easy to navigate. Most of our authors are drawn from Magic Circle and other top commercial firms, both in the United Kingdom and internationally.

Our titles are carefully produced, with the utmost attention paid to editorial, design and production processes. We hope this results in high-quality publications that are easy to read and a pleasure to own.

In 2021, we were very pleased to announce the start of a new chapter for Globe Law and Business following the acquisition of law books under the imprint Ark Publishing. Our law firm management list is now significantly expanded with many well-known and loved Ark Publishing titles.

We have also launched an online content platform, Globe Law Online, which allows for easy access across firms. Details of all titles included can be found at www.globelawonline.com. Email glo@globelawandbusiness.com for further details and to arrange a free trial for you or your firm.

We'd very much like to hear from you with your thoughts and ideas for improving what we offer. Please do feel free to email me at sian@globelawandbusiness.com. Happy reading and thank you for your time.

Sian O'Neill
Managing director
Globe Law and Business
www.globelawandbusiness.com

Patrick Smith
Senior staff writer, *The American Lawyer*
patricksmith8488@gmail.com

Patrick Smith is the senior staff writer for *The American Lawyer*, covering the business of law as it pertains to talent, growth, leadership and corporate work. He joined ALM in 2019, previously covering business, sports and crime at NY1, the *New York Daily News*, NBC Sports and The Bridge. He won an Emmy for his coverage of the 2016 Summer Olympics in Rio.

Patrick is a University of Illinois graduate with advanced degrees in international relations (Johns Hopkins University) and journalism (Columbia University). Prior to his time in media, he worked in both tech and the arts. He resides in Manhattan's Lower East Side.

Carlyn Kolker
Freelance writer and editor
carlyn.kolker@gmail.com

Carlyn Kolker is a freelance writer and editor based in Brooklyn, New York. She spent 15 years reporting on legal affairs and the business of law as a staff reporter at publications including *The American Lawyer*, Bloomberg News and Reuters, covering high-profile law firm mergers, white collar crime, securities law and changing law firm compensation systems. She is an adjunct lecturer of English at the City University of New York.

Table of contents

Introduction

In a rapidly changing competitive environment, many larger and more profitable law firms are experiencing outsized year-over-year growth relative to competitors, allowing them to pull further ahead of the pack over time. As a result, Big Law is undergoing an unprecedented shift: a relatively small number of top-performing firms across many peer groups are reaching new heights, which gives them an advantage in attracting talent and, consequently, clients and work. Meanwhile, other firms – historically rivals – risk falling behind.

The 2008 financial crisis, the rise of private capital and the unprecedented spike in global M&A in 2021 during the COVID-19 pandemic have had a profound impact on the legal industry. Most national and international law firms based in the United States and the United Kingdom achieved increased revenue and profits during this period, with some firms pulling away dramatically.

A group of outperforming firms, many of which we focus on in this book, far outpaced their peers in terms of revenue growth and profitability, driven in part by buoyant alternative asset classes such as private equity and private credit, increased large-scale M&A activity and high-stakes disputes. The dynamics at the very top of the market apply conceptually to other segments, albeit on a relative basis.

Some firms that successfully invested in building dominant market leadership in less rate-constrained areas of rapidly growing demand have recently been able to drive outsized increases in profit and revenue. As examples of rapid demand growth areas that produce sophisticated work, think of the intersection of energy, infrastructure, data centres and M&A, or of healthcare and private equity.

Firms have long competed against each other for talent, but the growing gap in size and profitability between competitors for that talent has dramatically increased the headwinds faced by smaller and less profitable firms across peer groups – their larger and more profitable rivals generally have greater flexibility on compensation, particularly for partners and groups of partners who generate disproportionate revenue for their firms.

This phenomenon is affecting firms of all sizes and profitability levels. Larger and more profitable firms develop distinct advantages that increase as the differential grows, creating an existential threat for others and leading some to lose their independence.

These headwinds are affecting even famous firms, such as some Wall Street firms that have rarely, if ever, experienced such challenges.

High-performing, sought-after partners want to be compensated in a manner they believe is fair – that is, at or close to the level they can command on the open market. They also want to be part of a winning team in their field, and a surefire way to achieve that is to join a market

Firms have long competed against each other for talent, but the growing gap in size and profitability between competitors for that talent has dramatically increased the headwinds faced by smaller and less profitable firms across peer groups.

leader that competes with rivals on size and profitability, generally leading to more interesting and rewarding work.

Throughout this book, we will examine how some firms have effectively positioned themselves to navigate this period of significant disruption and transition in the legal industry.

In the increasingly competitive hunt for talent, firms are grappling with matters such as their approach to compensation, strategic growth, competitive scale and profitability, expansion into new practices and geographies, changing partnership structures, leadership and succession planning, and the growing advantages of a high-performing team of business professionals, among other key elements.

With data and firsthand accounts from prominent leaders of a sample of firms that are thoughtfully navigating routes to outperformance, we will explore recent changes in the competitive landscape and explain what is on the horizon for the large group of firms affected by these changes, as well as the common drivers of success among firms that outperform their peers.

Acknowledgements
Undertaking a long-term project of any kind requires a village. This book was no different.

We would first like to thank all of the Big Law leaders who were willing to donate their time, expertise, insight and humour to this project. They are: Jon Ballis, Neil Barr, LeeAnn Black, Karen Braun, Ira Coleman, Brian Fahrney, Brad Karp, Alden Millard, Tim Mungovan, Andrew Nussbaum, Yvette Ostolaza, Bill Savitt and Mitch Zuklie.

We hope to talk with many more for future projects.

As with most things, a lot of work and support is done behind the scenes. We would like to thank the Zeughauser Group team for their support including Sadie Baron, Andrew Csensits, Bill Gelnaw, Alex Dimitrief, John Miller, Paul Pearlman, Jack Walker, Nolan Whitely, Mary K Young and Peter Zeughauser. We would also like to thank ALM for their support, and our families, who gave us grace as we worked on this project: Grace, Zoë and Xander Zimmermann; Troy, Caleb and Zeke Phipps; and Holly Hart and Adam Smith. Our village.

From all of us, thank you for your support in bringing this book to light. No one goes far alone, and your collective support and patience were the engine that made this project possible and kept it moving forward.

Kent, Patrick and Carlyn

I. A rapidly changing competitive landscape

1. Introduction

Consider a patient who needs specialised heart surgery. He or she wants a surgeon who is known as the best, or among the best, and who performs that work all day, every day, backed by a hospital with deep expertise and the resources to match. That hospital will be *the* leader in its field, and will be in high demand for the specialised heart surgery, drawing graduates focused on the same discipline who clamour to train there.

Now, apply these same advantages of market leadership, particularly at scale, to law firms. A law firm benefits from a deep bench of partners who are recognised as leaders in areas for which the firm wants to be known as the best, or one of the best.

This reputation attracts both talent and clients: lawyers want to learn from the best, and clients shortlist firms dominant in particular areas.

As demand increases, the firm is in a position to hold rates firm and increase them more rapidly than competitors, particularly in areas of practice experiencing growing demand. The result is a virtuous circle: market leadership drives increased demand, increased demand justifies premium rates, and profitability funds investment in the firm's people to defend or enhance its leadership position.

Almost all law firms are confronting a growing differential in both size and profitability relative to their competitors, and in recent years a small cohort of high-performing firms have pulled away from the pack at the top of the market.

But sustaining this advantage requires difficult decisions about growth priorities and change.

2. Growing differentials

As outperforming law firms grow in size and profitability, their relative ability to attract and retain needle-moving lawyers often expands. Over time, this creates substantial gaps in capability, depth of bench strength and market competitiveness between firms that were once similar.

Alden Millard, the chair of New York-based Simpson Thacher & Bartlett, comments as follows:[1]

> *I think a lot of the change in the industry is because there used to be a manageable differential between one firm and another firm that was a little bit bigger and higher performing. But as the differential grows, it becomes imperative for firms to do new things.*

Almost all law firms are confronting a growing differential in both size and profitability relative to their competitors, and in recent years a small cohort of high-performing firms have pulled away from the pack at the top of the market.

Two law firms in particular, Kirkland & Ellis and Latham & Watkins, are frequently cited for having reshaped the dynamics of revenue and profit growth, and now consistently take the top two spots on *The American Lawyer*'s list of highest-grossing firms, while also consistently being among the most profitable.[2] Those firms unseated the prior leaders on size from the 2000s and early 2010s, such as DLA Piper, Baker McKenzie and Jones Day.

Latham & Watkins first topped the Am Law 100 gross revenue rankings in the 2015 list. Then, two years later, Kirkland, with deep roots in the private equity sector, topped the list – a position it has held ever since – including in the latest rankings published in 2025, when it reported nearly $9 billion in gross revenue. Both firms are now achieving at least 1.5 times the revenue of their nearest competitors.

Other firms that have steadily climbed the Am Law 100 ranking, such as Ropes & Gray and Sidley Austin, have been propelled by premium work in powerful asset classes, including M&A and fund formation, as well as deal work for private equity and private credit firms.

Figure 1: Growing delta among Am Law 20 firms in gross revenue segments

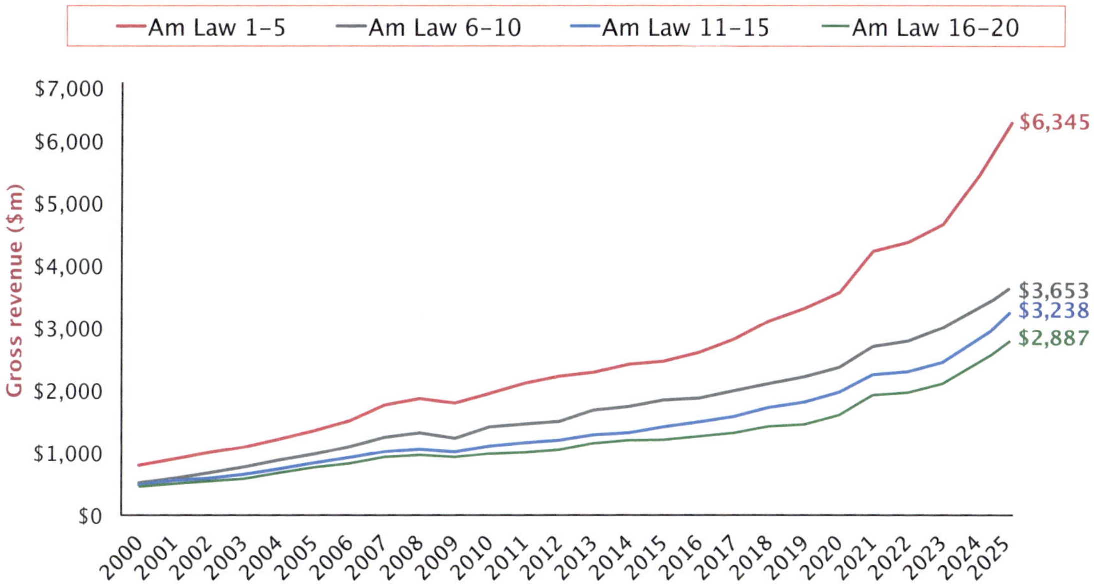

Source: Authors' own creation based on Am Law data.[3]

3. Size differentiation

Several firms with high gross revenue and headcount also boast high profitability. In contrast, in previous decades, firms that ranked high on the Am Law 100 list of highest-grossing revenue firms were not necessarily among the most profitable.

Firm leaders, particularly those in historically stable, venerated, Wall

Street-centric firms, often operated on the assumption that firms had to choose between profitability and size. However, more recently, a cohort of large and rapidly growing firms have turned that notion on its head. These firms have simultaneously expanded their headcount and gross revenue, while also increasing their profitability, some to levels that would not have sounded plausible just a few years ago. Many of these fast-growing firms are adding to headcount in high-revenue and profit-producing markets. For example, the majority of the most profitable firms are based in New York or have grown their New York offices to be their largest.

Latham & Watkins surpassed 800 attorneys in its New York office, more than 2.5 times as many as it had in its founding city, Los Angeles.[4]

Kirkland & Ellis, founded in Chicago, surpassed 1,000 lawyers in New York, making that office more than 20% larger than its Chicago office.[5]

4. Profitability gap

We also continue to observe a notable differential between Am Law 20 firms and other firms, as measured by profits per equity partner. Outperforming firms have shown a combination of approaches to growing their profitability.

Some firms focus their time and money on clients willing to pay premium rates, and leverage their strengths, particularly in areas of growing demand in which they can credibly become a market leader or defend their position as one, thereby adding to their ability to drive outsized revenue and profitability growth relative to other firms, all things being equal.

Some create a tier of non-equity partners, helping to retain the best associates without making them equity partners; cull underperforming partners with discipline; and pair strategic headcount growth with ambitious rate increases.

Some pick up the pace on strategic growth with groups of laterals.

And some firms do all these things and more, as we will explore.

Figure 2: Growing delta between Am Law 200 firms and others in profits per equity partner

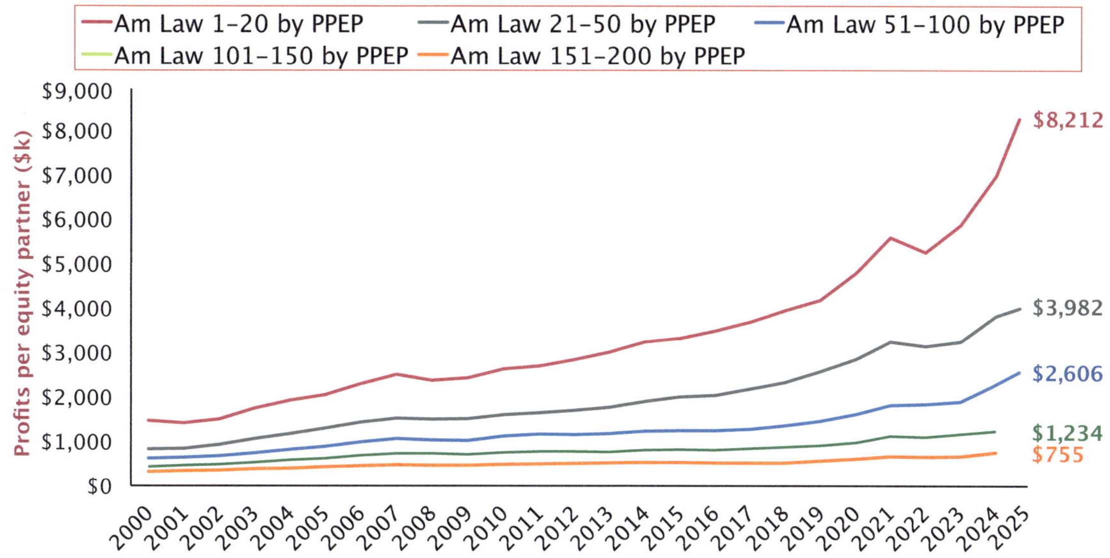

5. Increasing stratification

A trend of increasing stratification is becoming evident even among the most profitable firms. Some firms – call them 'the elite of the elite' – are pulling away from the pack. There is a growing gap in profitability between the elite performers and the next tranche of high-performing firms.

Figure 3: Gap between the top five most profitable firms and the next five firms, as measured by PPEP

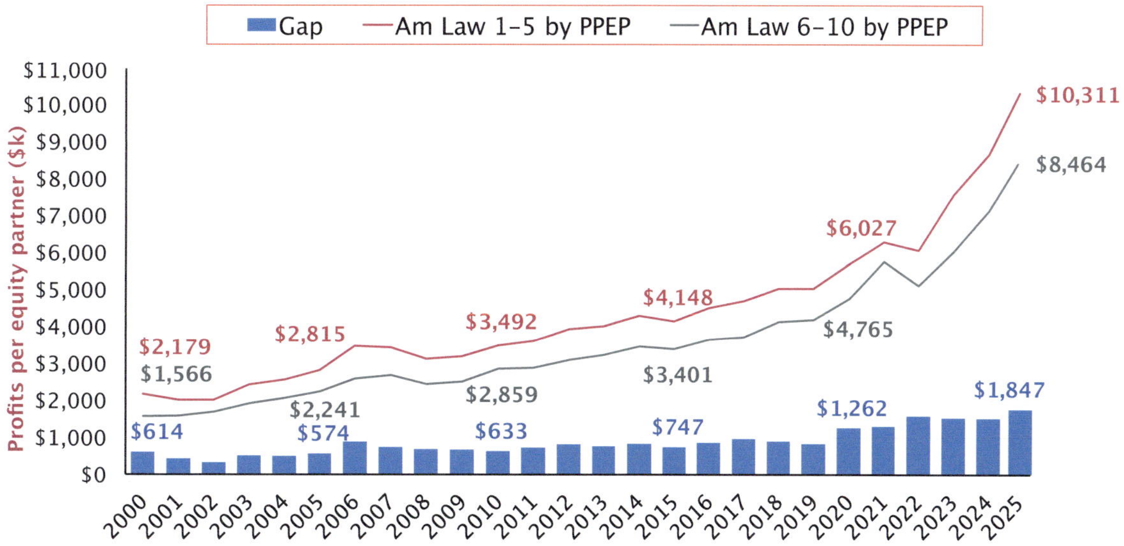

A fundamental truth emerged from our work and the input we received from leaders of outperforming firms: most have no desire to become a different firm, but they do aspire to be a stronger version of themselves.

6. The magnet of outperformance
Simply put, outperformance relative to direct competitors for talent enables firms to more often attract more desirable lawyers and clients.

Market dominance creates a strong magnet for sought-after clients, work and talent. Given that outperforming firms have comparatively greater resources to invest in talent, more ability to leverage their deeper bench, and the capacity to make larger capital investments, these firms are well positioned to ascend to ever greater heights, making them hard to keep up with.

To provide a data point, many high-performing firms invest 1% of their gross revenue annually in capital expenditure – referred to in some firms as R&D – focusing on:

- technology and innovation broadly;
- leveraging the firm's knowledge and other information;
- data analytics;
- practice leadership development; and
- broader talent development.

One per cent of $500 million is $5 million; of $1 billion is $10 million; of $3 billion is $30 million; and of $9 billion is $90 million.

These are substantial annual investments.

7. Specialisation
General counsel and business leaders who select outside firms report in surveys that they frequently turn to just a shortlist of firms for board-level matters in whatever areas of legal expertise they need, whether that's high-stakes transactional, litigation or regulatory work.

This creates potential advantages for firms in prioritising growth in certain practices, sectors and cities. For example, it may mean focusing on certain sub-areas of high-stakes litigation, such as mass tort litigation and certain transactional matters, including large-scale M&A, to meet the seemingly insatiable needs of private equity and alternative asset funds to deploy capital and generate higher returns.

In addition to Kirkland and Latham, other highly profitable firms that have differentiated themselves in these areas include Paul, Weiss, Rifkind, Wharton & Garrison, Proskauer Rose and Sidley, to name a few – all firms whose rates of growth in revenue and profitability over the last decade have exceeded the norm.

This work is also driving firms to merge or look for acquisition opportunities to accelerate achievement of their goals on size, profitability and market leadership in chosen areas. McDermott Will & Emery's 2025 merger with Schulte Roth & Zabel – a firm with deep ties to hedge funds and private capital clients – to become McDermott Will & Schulte, is one of the latest and highest-profile examples of how firms are thinking big, and fast forwarded the achievement of their aspirations with inorganic growth. We will discuss this combination in more depth in Chapter VI, "Strategic M&A: accelerating the plan".

8. Vulnerabilities

Firms that have slipped on a relative basis, allowing a growing gap in size and profitability compared to competitors, have less flexibility on compensation, making them more vulnerable to losing key partners, which can in turn trigger a loss of independence.

A trickle of high-performing partners departing can become a stream, sparking a crisis of confidence in leadership. Such crises are a common thread in the narratives of firms that experienced reversals of fortune, lost their independence or dissolved.

In New York, for example, firms that lost their independence in recent years suffered from this growing differential in size and profitability relative to their closest competitors. These included Stroock & Stroock & Lavan (now dissolved), Shearman & Sterling (now A&O Shearman following its 2024 merger with Allen & Overy), Kramer Levin Naftalis & Frankel (now Herbert Smith Freehills Kramer following its 2025 merger with Herbert Smith Freehills), and Schulte Roth & Zabel (now McDermott Will & Schulte following the 2025 merger referred to above).

A similar story played out earlier in Texas, where national and multinational firms that leveraged size and profitability advantages poached needle-moving partners from regional players in the late 2010s and early 2020s, resulting in a loss of independence for firms such as Gardere Wynne Sewell (now part of Foley & Lardner following their 2018 merger), Thompson & Knight (now Holland & Knight following their 2021 merger), and Andrews Kurth Kenyon (now Hunton Andrews Kurth following its 2018 merger with Hunton & Williams).

While each firm's transition has its own unique story, all suffered from major and growing gaps in scale and profitability compared to larger competitors. This made it difficult for them to match compensation levels and invest sufficiently in the future of their firms, and ultimately reduced their appeal to both talent and clients.

In the chapters that follow we will examine those firms that have outperformed, and how they have done so, with particular focus on the drivers of their success and what can be learned from them by other firms. Conversely, we look at the perils many firms face by not making certain choices, and acting on them, to stay in the same league as their historical and aspirational competitors on a long-term basis.

A fundamental truth emerged from our work and the input we received from leaders of outperforming firms: most have no desire to become a different firm, but they do aspire to be a stronger version of themselves. A firm that is performing well in isolation may still be weakening within the competitive landscape. Relative comparison is essential, given that firms are competing for talent.

The cost of staying the course or doing nothing differently – even when a firm is improving in absolute terms – can be substantial.

Notes

1 The authors wish to thank the many contributors who shared their comments and insights in interviews for this Special Report.
2 Rankings, lists and other data throughout this Special Report, unless otherwise indicated, are from Am Law (*The American Lawyer*, Law.com), with permission.
3 Throughout this Special Report, graph data is calculated by taking the average of each segment on a year-by-year basis. Firms switching between segments are counted based on which one they were grouped with in each given year.
4 ALM data, Law.com Compass.
5 *Ibid.*

II. The benefits of competitive scale and profitability

1. Introduction

Simultaneously growing scale relative to competitors, while also enhancing profitability and achieving dominant market leadership, can create a significant competitive advantage for law firms, in terms of both talent and clients. Over the last decade, in an environment where more and more high-performing firms are able to grow these elements simultaneously and at impressive speed year over year, competitive scale has become widely understood to be a key ingredient of outperformance.

Competitive scale and profitability relative to competitors often yield a talent advantage. This creates advantages in competing for clients and work, which in turn means greater flexibility in keeping up with, or even setting, the market for compensation for desirable people and teams. Competitive scale and profitability are also frequent precursors to picking spots to dominate as a market leader.

This generates the resources to build extensive depth of quality, and to raise the firm's profile, in these spots, offering the firm a welcome flow of clients, work, and people. Clients and lawyers alike are attracted to a winning team that is recognised as a safe choice in the sectors and practices in which it aspires to be a market leader.

The laws of scale, leading to a compounding effect, allow firms to transform annual rate increases into a swift and powerful revenue engine. This helps firms pull away from competitors. A 10% increase in billing rates for a $500 million firm would yield an additional $50 million in revenue in a single year. That same increase would give a $5 billion firm another $500 million.

Figure 1: Larger firms leverage the impact of compounding

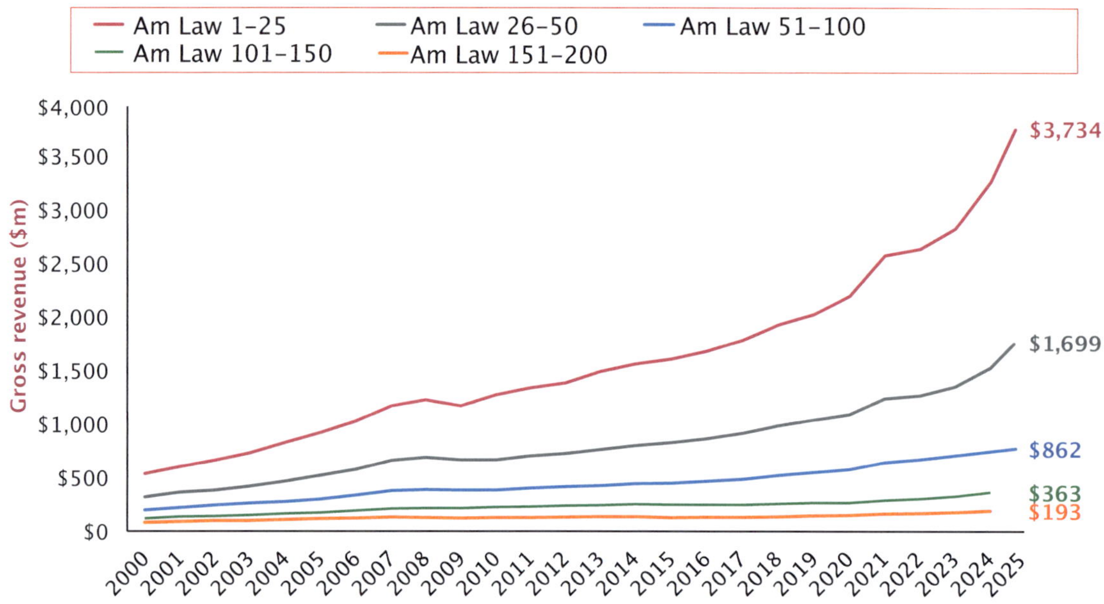

That additional money, which translates into considerable additional profit at well-managed firms, can then be allocated back to the partnership. It can also be used to mark compensation to market as the market moves upward for existing high-performing partners and prospective partners.

In addition, it can also afford the firm the opportunity to invest more in high-impact technologies, data analytics and other innovations, and to deepen the firm's bench of quality in areas of focus to capture greater market share.

Indeed, the revenue trajectory of the Am Law 200 demonstrates the strength of scaling up. From 2015 to 2025, different segments of the Am Law 200 experienced diverging growth paths, with the top 25 firms growing at 2.2 times the rate of the firms in the Am Law 50 to 200 ranking.

2. "Additive ... not core"

While scale can be both a driver and an outcome of success, it does not necessarily guarantee it.

Perhaps no law firm leader has articulated the advantages of scale better than Jon Ballis, chairman of Kirkland & Ellis, a firm that has achieved market-leading scale:

> *Once you have scale, there are certain things you are then able to do, and we have tried to make ourselves better because of the scale we have. So, it is additive, but it is not core. It's an enhancer. It's like a flavoring to a soup. It's not the base.*

Figure 2: Different segments of the Am Law 200 experienced diverging growth paths

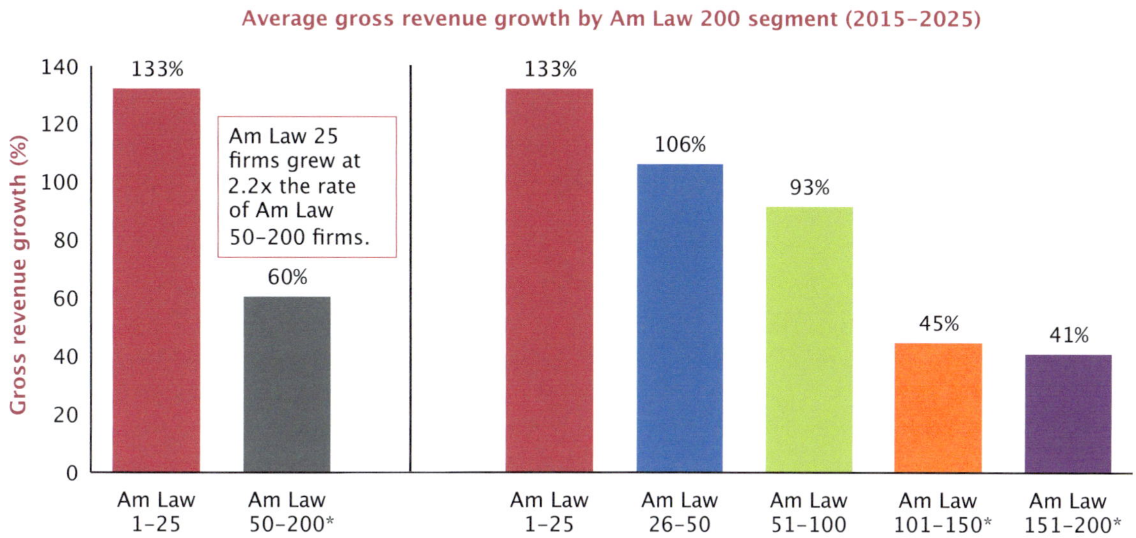

* Am Law 50–200, 101–150 and 151–200 represent 2014–2024 growth rates due to lack of publicly available FY25 data for the second hundred.

Outperforming firms increasingly think in terms of balancing the benefits of scale with those of competitive profitability, depth of quality and its consistency, and ensuring a high-performing culture that aligns with the requirements to advance the firm's strategy.

At its heart, competitive scale feeds a firm's ability to compound its growth year over year for the long term. From the perspective of firms that are undersized relative to competitors, a manageable differential in size and/or profitability can quickly grow into a less manageable one, thereby creating competitive disadvantages and threats.

In this chapter we examine how, all things being equal, greater scale and profitability create a talent advantage. This typically leads to a client advantage, particularly for firms that prioritise growth of deeper and higher-profile market leadership in specific areas:

- those that extend existing strengths;
- those that are areas of growing demand; and
- those in which the firm can command its rates.

At its heart, competitive scale feeds a firm's ability to compound its growth year over year for the long term. From the perspective of firms that are undersized relative to competitors, a manageable differential in size and/or profitability can quickly grow into a less manageable one, thereby creating competitive disadvantages and threats.

We also hear from the leaders of several high-performing firms that have evaluated their firm's scale and profitability relative to competitors and have made strategic choices about how to manage the differential.

3. Scale as a balancing act

Neil Barr, chair of Davis Polk & Wardwell, considers his firm's optimal scale by examining its position relative to competitors. The group of firms against which Davis Polk competes has expanded beyond the elite New York firms with comparable performance metrics that it once regarded as its traditional competitors. The competitive landscape now includes firms such as Kirkland & Ellis and Latham & Watkins, which have leveraged considerable scale to their advantage:

> *I'm trying to make sure that each of our core practices is scaled to a competitive positioning with our competitors. It doesn't have to be the same size. It has to be a competitive positioning. Then we will let the brand and quality do the balance of the work.*

Recent efforts to address this competitive positioning have been paying off: in 2025, Davis Polk grew its gross revenue by 25.98% to $3.20 billion and its profits per equity partner by 25.64% to $9.8 million.

Barr's point about brand and quality underscores a key concept central to firms' desire to grow in scale: scale becomes more powerful when it is accompanied by simultaneous growth in profitability, quality and market leadership, without disrupting the best of the firm's culture.

Some of these attributes are intangibles that can drive perception of a firm's brand in the marketplace. Brand perception can drive both clients and talent to a firm or send them in the other direction. A firm known to clients for excellence in specific practice areas will be even better regarded if it maintains its quality as it expands. If it can't maintain the consistency of its quality, so goes its reputation.

Barr focuses on this balancing act as he assesses his firm's position within its competitive landscape:

> *We are not yet optimized in some of our offices. We may need to scale further just to remain competitive. For our firm, which is so culturally oriented and focused on the quality of service, there is a trade-off with the marginal unit of growth: cultural dilution and brand dilution. And so I think that we have our eye on it as a question, but not a foregone conclusion.*

As a key player in capital markets and M&A transactions, Davis Polk, with just under 200 partners, competes with much larger firms, prompting Barr to examine how to grow his firm through lateral hiring, a subject we'll delve into in more detail in Chapter V, "Lateral hires and teams: accelerating the strategy". By contrast, Latham & Watkins's equity partnership is about five times the size of Davis Polk's, and Kirkland & Ellis's is some nine times larger, according to 2025 Am Law data.[1] However, the three firms are much closer in their profits per equity partner, as reported by Am Law.

Takeaway: Davis Polk's experience demonstrates that balancing scale, culture and profitability relative to competitors is an imperative for many outperforming firms.

4. When size matters less

Some firms – such as litigation, IP and sometimes transactional boutiques – may not grow their size as much. Many of these firms focus their practice more narrowly than larger firms, while seeking a competitive advantage based on consistent top-quality results and, by extension, their brand.

This path can lead to sustainable competitive advantage, but with limited scale. In other words, winning on profitability and dominant market leadership can sometimes compensate for lack of size relative to larger rivals, at least to a degree.

A prime example of a market-leading firm of limited size relative to many or most of its rivals is Wachtell, Lipton, Rosen & Katz. The firm, to which its clients turn for board-level, often bet-the-company transactions and disputes, is the smallest firm in the Am Law 20, with approximately 80 equity partners as of the end of 2025.[2]

For Wachtell, extreme attention to quality, profitability and a market-leading brand in carefully chosen areas of focus means that turning away work – and a lot of it – is a prerequisite for dominating in select areas for which it can command premium rates, as co-chairs Andrew Nussbaum and Bill Savitt explain. According to Nussbaum:

> *I do think there's an ethos of the kind of work we want to do and how we want to do it, the impact we believe lawyers can and should have when practicing at the highest level. To maintain the kind of profitability that we have and the premium reputation that we have, there's a lot of work we shouldn't do, and you need to be willing to say, gee, this one doesn't seem good for us. Being busy is not a goal; being busy on the most challenging and complex work is.*

Savitt echoes Nussbaum's point, noting that the firm's ability to remain small yet high-performing stems in part from its selectivity in the work it undertakes. The more selective a firm is, he says, the more likely it is to stay within its niche and maintain limited scale while remaining highly profitable and consistently outperforming:

> *It's important to us to avoid a situation where we don't have enough premium work to keep our lawyers fully occupied. Because in that scenario, there would be pressure to take on work we don't want or is not that interesting to our people. That has never been our approach. We instead have always stayed small and focused and turned down work, to be sure we are doing the things we are best at. And it's a choice that has enormous implications for growth and breadth of practice and billing.*

As observers of law firms for decades, we would strongly concur with Savitt's insight. For many firms, to act on this advice – Savitt did not say it directly, but we will – would mean making hard choices to address chronic overcapacity, meaning counselling out lawyers, and in some cases groups of lawyers, or even entire practices and offices for some firms, that have chronically underperformed their partnership's expectations for years without a good reason.

Savitt states that, given his firm's model, growth at scale is not the best option for him and his partners:

> *I think it would be really hard for us to do what we're trying to do and be in the niche that we're trying to have and have the reputation we want if we found ourselves with lots of lawyers but not enough of the kind of premium work we aim to do. That would become a problem.*

Takeaway: Wachtell's experience is consistent with the fact that, for many firms that would like to outperform peers on profitability with limited scale, a key ingredient of success is to have strategically chosen, relatively narrow areas of focus, accompanied by a disciplined commitment to concentrating only on clients and matters that drive profitability relative to competitors, and for which the firm most wants to be known, while often passing on other opportunities.

5. Leveraging scale

At the other end of the size spectrum from Wachtell is Kirkland. Its trajectory over the last twenty years shows growth in scale unmatched in the history of law firms, with simultaneous market-leading profitability.

In 2005, the firm ranked 9th in the Am Law 100 rankings for gross revenue and 7th for profits per equity partner. At that time, Kirkland was not among the small group of firms shattering the $1 billion mark in gross revenue.[3] But twenty years later it is a hegemon, with more than $10 billion in annual revenue and more than $11 million in profits per equity partner, ranking first in the former and second in the latter (to Wachtell) according to the most recent Am Law data.[4]

These results are the payoff for the firm's decades-long strategy to increase both revenue and profitability through targeted expansion in areas of strategic priority, often with a focus on strengthening existing client relationships.

The firm now has over 4,000 lawyers (and counting) and has grown far beyond its Chicago roots, with offices that are among the largest of any law firm in the world's top financial centres, such as New York and London, and in other key financial and commercial centres in the United States, Europe, Asia and the Middle East.

Much of the firm's success is driven by a decision to expand market leadership in areas of strength, resulting in a disciplined focus on building extensive depth of quality and profile in areas for which the firm seeks to be known as dominant.

Historically, these areas have included private equity, bankruptcy and restructuring, and high-stakes litigation, although the list has expanded over the years. Not only has the firm built a position of market leadership in these areas and commanded rates that enhance its profitability, but the firm's areas of focus create a balanced portfolio of practices that help to mitigate the risks of market volatility. The firm is hedged between cyclical practices (such as private equity), and acyclical (such as sophisticated litigation) and counter-cyclical work (such as bankruptcy and restructuring). This has allowed the firm to perform more consistently through the ups and downs of market cycles.

Many market observers credit Kirkland partner Jack Levin – who, at the time of writing, is 89 and still attends annual partner gatherings – with being a leading pioneer who made private equity the powerful force it is today. It allowed the firm to have considerable first-mover advantage in the space, and it has ridden a massive wave since then.

Kirkland started by focusing on funds outside the bulge bracket, then maintained and grew those relationships while also developing strong relationships with bulge bracket funds. This has created an additional hedge: the firm performs well whether mid-sized transactions predominate or large deals are more plentiful.

In 2023 and 2024, the firm ranked first as a mergers and acquisitions adviser on the largest deals, according to London Stock Exchange

Group rankings.[5] The firm is perennially in the top five for both deal value and volume.

But according to Jon Ballis, it's not enough to look at the growth of Kirkland's headcount, revenue and profits. He is also keenly aware that Kirkland's immense scale confers additional, material advantages:

> *There's no secret sauce, but there are a few key attributes. We know how to hire laterally, and we know how to leverage our platform really well.*

We will discuss Kirkland's approach to lateral hiring in more detail in Chapter V, "Lateral hires and teams: accelerating the strategy". But it is interesting to hear Ballis's views on the concrete benefits provided to his firm by scale. He uses a tasty analogy to describe it:

> *I think I'd say the benefits of scale are, if we're doing the ice cream sundae analogy, the benefits of scale are not the ice cream. It's maybe not the cherry on top, but it's either the chocolate sauce or the whipped cream. It makes it better.*

One big cherry on top is the firm's ability to invest in what Ballis describes as R&D. "We spend about 1% of our revenue per year on

"I think I'd say the benefits of scale are, if we're doing the ice cream sundae analogy, the benefits of scale are not the ice cream. It's maybe not the cherry on top, but it's either the chocolate sauce or the whipped cream. It makes it better."

Jon Ballis, chairman, Kirkland & Ellis

new initiatives," he explains, referring to these initiatives as R&D, a term not widely used by law firms in reference to their firm. Others often call it CapEx, but Ballis's terminology shows how he thinks about investment in the firm's present and future competitiveness, and why Kirkland benefits from having more to spend than any other firm as a percentage of revenue. And no firm has had more revenue than Kirkland in recent years.

While 1% may not seem significant, it actually represents a substantial investment. Given that the firm generated over $10 billion in revenue in 2025, a 1% allocation would equate to approximately $100 million annually. This funding could be directed toward investments in areas such as data and analytics, technology and other initiatives aimed at enhancing the firm's value to key clients, strengthening and expanding those relationships, and attracting new clients.

"We invest heavily in what we call knowledge management. All firms have it," says Ballis. At Kirkland, knowledge management (KM) comprises a robust operation and far bigger area of investment than in most firms. "We have three equity partners and about 15 to 20 income partners," he says, "who do not have a practice and focus full time on this." He points out that these are not lawyers who didn't make it in practice, noting that some make seven figures.

While these partners do not directly generate revenue by practising law, Ballis explains, their value is derived from their ability to identify and harness data and knowledge about the firm's work in given areas. This creates advantages for the firm in terms of growing the size and value of existing relationships and generating new ones.

"We've built internal systems where we track all of the deals we do," Ballis explains. "Scale helps with that." Greater depth of quality, he says, leads to greater market leadership which leads to a larger flow of transactions, and data about them.

Ballis illustrates the strength of the KM group's work with a compelling vignette from the early 2020s. He was asked to attend a pitch meeting to expand an existing client relationship of strategic importance to the firm.

> *We meet with a very large, top five private equity firm with which we have a good relationship but for which we were not doing a lot of fund formation. I go there as a very senior person in the firm and explain: "We do a lot of work with you. We don't do this part. We'd love to do it. We think we can do a very good job."*

After a few words from a leader of the firm's fund formation practice, a KM partner took the lead on the rest of the pitch. This would be unusual in most firms. What happened next, led by the KM partner, is, as Ballis tells the story, what won the firm the fund formation work it was pursuing.

The KM partner used anonymised Kirkland data about other funds it had formed for other clients to show the unusually high level of value the firm could provide, given the very large trove of data it had collected and analysed. According to Ballis, the KM partner explained as follows:

> *Look, I've taken your fund document. You were kind enough to provide it to us confidentially. I've mapped it against the top 25 clients we have on a blind basis. Here's the thing. I've mapped it against 75 key terms. And I can't tell you which of the firms did what, but here's the anonymized chart that shows you on a graph where you guys are fitting in.*

Next, the KM partner showed a version of the client's terms, colour-coded in green, yellow and red. Green indicated the client's terms were best of breed based on all of Kirkland's data about terms of other funds; yellow meant there was room for improvement; and red meant the client's terms were off-market and should be improved. The partner then demonstrated how Kirkland could provide additional

Firms that leverage economies of scale to make significant investments can develop competitive advantages and achieve substantial rewards.

valuable data and corresponding clauses for the fund to incorporate into its fund formation documents.

The result was stunning, Ballis said:

> *[The KM partner] just won us $20 million of business. So that's amazing. One thing that scale provides, for sure, is that it allows for data and investment. It's really R&D. We are investing today for future success.*

Takeaway: Firms that leverage economies of scale to make significant investments can develop competitive advantages and achieve substantial rewards. This strategy allows them to build larger and more profitable relationships with key clients, securing a greater share of their spending on outside counsel, often at higher rates over time. As revenue increases, this approach not only boosts profits but also helps firms gain greater market share in their targeted practices and sectors.

6. Scale brings complexity

Of course, scale also brings a level of complexity for firms to manage. The larger a business, the greater the complexity.

"There are costs to scale," Ballis observes. "And so, we have exchange rate complications. We have international tax optimization concerns, transfer pricing analyses – it's complicated."

LeeAnn Black, chief operating officer of Latham & Watkins, which has about 3,700 lawyers spread across 14 countries, navigates the complexities of scale every day:

> *You wake up every morning, and there's any number of things going on at the firm and more generally in the world, and you have to know how to digest that and get people to stay calm and prioritize and do what needs to be done.*

Black explains how 'what needs to be done' can range from a lateral group being integrated into the firm, to an earthquake occurring on the other side of the country, to an international political crisis erupting across the world.

For example, given Latham's roots, the Los Angeles wildfires in January 2025 hit particularly close to home. Black had a team in place, focused on ensuring that the firm's personnel (including retired partners and clients) were safe and supported, both during the fires and in the months that followed, as colleagues rebuilt or relocated. According to Black:

We wanted to be sure our people knew we were there for them every step of the way, first and foremost from a basic safety perspective, but also when it came to well-being support, assistance with temporary housing and insurance claims, and (if needed) financial support from LathamCares.[6]

She adds the following:

You have to have really strong quality and talent throughout the organization, because you can't rely on five people to get everything done. You have to have all the pieces in place to train and get people to the level that you need them to be, so that they can be out in front, performing in ways that continuously improve how you serve your clients and your business. It's also about putting processes in place that allow you to scale.

7. Innovating scale

In terms of process, LeeAnn Black sees AI as the next tool to help large firms scale, noting that Latham is already investing in and customising new products in the space:

We're seeing ways in which we can do things much more efficiently and effectively. That should bolster our ability to scale. We're also focused on helping our clients as they navigate the AI landscape in their own businesses – it's a unique time for nearly every industry and profession, and we realize that our firm and our industry is just one of many grappling with these fast-moving changes.

Mitch Zuklie, chair of Orrick, Herrington & Sutcliffe, also notes that innovation is central to his firm's culture and its long-term strategy:

Having powerful data is everything. That suggests you want to focus on particular markets, achieve distinctive scale in those markets, gather data that's accurate and be able to mine that data and synthesize it for clients in a relevant way.

Firms that have vast troves of data about work they do in areas of strategic focus for important clients will have a leg up in using AI, Zuklie predicts:

In the disruption that we all face from AI, scale probably is an advantage. Imagine a company that has $2 billion of revenue or a company that has $10 billion of revenue, and you're each going to invest 1% of your revenue into technological innovation. Well, you can do an awful lot more with $100 million investment than with a $20 million investment. And I think that level of resource investment at a moment like now probably gives you a competitive advantage of finding something that's a meaningful, sustainable advantage.

The ability of select Big Law firms to harness data about the work they do in areas of focus, while balancing ethical obligations, mirrors the success of several Big Tech players, says Zuklie. For the most part, the so-called Magnificent Seven technology companies – a cohort of top tech companies by market cap – are, at heart, data companies that have, at the time of writing, seen extraordinary increases in value based on the combination of scale and data.

According to Zuklie:

> *If we become more data-driven organizations, we'll more closely replicate the benefits of these platforms. I think you need to have scale, but it has to be focused scale. So, the way I look at that is that it's a race to do several things: to have sufficient scale, to have it in relevant segments of the economy, capture the relevant data, and be able to grab that data, utilize it, and share it in a way that it's actionable. So, I think it's a race to do all of those things.*

Takeaway: With AI looming as both a threat and an opportunity for most law firms, some forward-thinking firms have already made strides in identifying, harvesting and using data about work they do. This is often employed in combination with innovative technology, particularly in areas of strategic focus and when the data advantages the firm in pitching and doing work for important clients. It is also useful in retaining and recruiting sought-after lawyers who prefer to be on a platform that has a deeper reservoir of relevant data that is valuable to their clients.

Notes

1 See Legal.io, "The 2025 Am Law 100: By the Numbers", 15 April 2025, www.legal.io/articles/5609720/The-2025-Am-Law-100-By-the-Numbers.
2 *Ibid.*
3 *Ibid.*
4 See Andrew Maloney, "$20M and Still Going: Is Partner Pay a Bubble", Law.com, 11 July 2024, www.law.com/americanlawyer/2024/07/11/20m-and-still-going-is-partner-pay-a-bubble/?slreturn=20260413095123.
5 LSE League Tables (law firm and investment banking) are available at: www.lseg.com/en/data-analytics/financial-data/deals-data/investment-banking-league-tables.
6 LathamCares is Latham's 501(c)(3) arm.

III. The value of a strategic plan

1. Introduction

In an environment where only a small subset of firms ascend to positions of truly dominant market leadership, bringing high-performing partners onto the same page about what success looks like for the firm over time – and developing a granular plan to get there – has been a valuable exercise for many outperforming firms in recent years.

Some firms begin this process from a position of strength, with partnership buy-in and resources available for the endeavour. Others start from a position of vulnerability, where a plan is something to steady a firm already losing its bearings.

Some organisations find themselves positioned between extremes. Effective development of a strategic plan begins with a deep dive into data about the firm and its competitive landscape, a candid SWOT assessment, determining the firm's strengths, weaknesses, opportunities and threats in relation to competitors. This process also typically includes one-on-one unattributed discussions with a sample of formal and informal leaders within the firm to gain insights into their vision for the firm's future and to understand what they believe is essential to achieving it.

In this chapter we examine how two firms, Simpson Thacher & Bartlett and Proskauer Rose, developed plans that have already yielded positive returns. For these firms, a defined strategic planning process enabled them to identify areas of practice and sectors where they could distinguish themselves favourably relative to their competitors for talent and clients.

We discuss their planning processes, and hear in their own words how the sheer act of going through the exercise helped them identify their future paths and energise the effort to successfully traverse them.

2. Starting from strength

When Alden Millard took the reins of Simpson Thacher in 2022, the firm had been showing strong performance for years. For example, when *The American Lawyer* reported on the firm's 2015 financial performance, revenues were $1.28 billion and profits per equity partner were $3.47 million.[1] By 2021, the firm's revenues had improved by nearly 75% to just over $2.2 billion and profits per equity partner had improved by more than 70% to nearly $6 million.[2]

Even with that degree of improved performance, soon after he became chair of the firm's executive committee, Millard decided that it would benefit the firm to build consensus on, and articulate a vision of, success for the firm's future and a granular plan to achieve it. Millard's desire was fuelled in part by his observation that competition for talent and clients in the marketplace had increased. And he sensed that certain firms achieving outsized success were doing so in a strategic and intentional manner.

> *It was clear to me that other firms were developing and executing defined growth strategies. So even though we had a strong tailwind, it was important that we conceptualize our plans and align our partnership around a shared plan for the future.*

Like other leaders of historically successful firms, Millard was observing macro trends in the marketplace that were prompting him to examine his firm's position. While it was clear that Simpson Thacher was continuing to grow rapidly in both size and profitability, fuelled by long-time market leadership in private equity and other areas, the firm's performance did not exist in a vacuum.

What was important was not just Simpson Thacher's consistently improving size and profitability in isolation, but its performance relative to competitors for sought-after lawyers, clients and work. In the minds of many law firm leaders, being competitive on relative size and profitability matters because it can drive greater flexibility on compensation – particularly among top revenue generators and rising stars.

In the minds of many law firm leaders, being competitive on relative size and profitability matters because it can drive greater flexibility on compensation – particularly among top revenue generators and rising stars.

With this in mind, Millard focused on managing the differential relative to competitors by accelerating strategic growth, maintaining elite-level profitability and building even more dominant market leadership and depth of quality in specific areas of focus.

Millard notes that by articulating a vision from a position of strength, Simpson Thacher was able to prioritise its investments at the crossroads of practices and sectors that were experiencing rising demand. This strategy not only leveraged Simpson Thacher's strengths but also created opportunities for significant revenue and profit growth. The move represented a notable shift for a firm that had historically excelled in its core work at the highest levels of the market.

The strategic plan marked a new way for the firm to adapt to a changing competitive landscape and prepare for the future. For Simpson Thacher, this was particularly significant as it was the first time in nearly a century and a half – the firm was founded in 1884 – that it had created and implemented a formal written strategic plan. The plan would outline a vision of future success, identify the firm's highest priorities to achieve it, and articulate how it would distinguish itself in the long term, complete with specific, measurable goals and a timeline for achievement.

"I was seeing several things that I thought we could do better, that we could execute on much more effectively," recalls Millard.

Leaders of some firms develop plans independently, whereas other leaders engage external strategic advisers. Simpson Thacher benefited from having an outside adviser with experience advising high-performing law firms in strategic planning. As Millard puts it, "Especially in the beginning, we would have just been stuck in neutral trying to figure out how to get started."

During the planning process, law firms often undertake an exercise to gain a deeper understanding of the factors that contribute to outperformance among relevant competitors. This involves analysing the historical compound annual growth rates of the firm and its peers in relation to key performance metrics. By forecasting future performance based on these historical growth rates, firms can obtain a clearer picture of how differences in size and profitability may change over time, assuming that past trends continue.

The analysis helps firms understand the potential impact of growing performance differentials on compensation flexibility and investment opportunities for the firm's future. This clarity, in turn, enables leadership to avoid complacency and fosters consensus on difficult strategic decisions – determining the necessary changes, how extensive they should be, and how to position the firm most effectively to attract and retain sought-after talent and clients.

By gaining insight into how other firms operate and the shifting dynamics of the competitive landscape, partners often realise that failing to create and execute a plan carries real costs. They may also discover that standing still weakens their position, particularly when rivals are advancing – sometimes from a higher baseline and at greater speed. Firms that don't improve performance while competitors make significant progress can fall behind. In a rapidly evolving market, even modest improvement can mean decline if competitors are moving faster.

Once armed with this and other detailed information about a firm and its competitive set, and with an opportunity to discuss it together, partners are often more willing to make the difficult decisions to get to the next level. This is particularly true when partners see the increased flexibility on compensation enjoyed by many firms as they develop greater scale and profitability.

Having a well-informed external adviser share best practices on how high-performing organisations have successfully climbed steep hills often inspires a growth mindset and greater consensus on goals and plan tactics. In addition, in the early part of planning, tapping an adviser who is independent of the partnership to conduct one-on-one unattributed consultations – to get candid input from partners who do not need to worry about sounding like outliers or having to defend their views – can often set the stage for broader buy-in for the plan that eventually comes out of the planning process.

Unattributed consultations can be instrumental in identifying points of consensus among key partners and highlighting areas where consensus needs to be built. Furthermore, these discussions often provide valuable insights into relevant data and the competitive landscape, which can enhance the planning process. Relying solely on a firm's internal views and data may yield less effective results.

Additionally, conducting unattributed interviews and clearly articulating the consensus among both formal and informal leaders can help a firm minimise the influence of individual outlier opinions. Such opinions can sometimes dominate discussions and derail progress, especially if they are expressed loudly. Early identification of consensus during planning can help guide the conversation back on track, ensuring that discussions remain focused and productive.

Conducting unattributed interviews and clearly articulating the consensus among both formal and informal leaders can help a firm minimise the influence of individual outlier opinions.

A clear and detailed understanding of the evolving competitive landscape is particularly valuable because influential partners are often focused primarily on their practice and may lack a sufficiently well-informed understanding of the relative level of performance their firm will require over time to remain optimally competitive in the talent market.

A clear and detailed understanding of the evolving competitive landscape is particularly valuable because influential partners are often focused primarily on their practice and may lack a sufficiently well-informed understanding of the relative level of performance their firm will require over time to remain optimally competitive in the talent market.

When partners see a preview of a draft plan before it is fully signed and sealed, they are often less likely to throw stones later in the process. Consulted from the get-go, they can't complain that "Nobody ever asked me for my views."

However, across high-performing law firms, it is common for different partners to reach strategic choices through the lens of their own experience. For many such choices – whether about growth priorities, how to balance culture with enhancing size and profitability, or anything else – it is often not feasible to please all partners. In this scenario, outperforming firms increasingly come to the view that it is in the firm's best interests to prioritise those high-performing partners the firm can least afford to lose.

At Simpson Thacher, an important early milestone in the planning process was the consensus reached – in a working group that included formal and informal leaders – as to a vision for the firm's future. A vision statement typically consists of a paragraph identifying what success looks like within three to five years – aspirational yet reasonably achievable, and distinguishing the firm from rivals through credible points of differentiation that the firm can sustain over time.

In Simpson Thacher's case, the vision articulated in the firm's plan underscores its aspiration to remain a long-term leader at the intersection of alternative asset management, M&A and finance. The firm identified seven specific practice groups to prioritise for growth over the planning horizon which would, in turn, inform the investment priorities in its strategic growth plan.

"The vision statement was incredibly helpful, both for getting us started and keeping us focused," Millard notes. "Putting it in print, in words, in charts, helped a lot."

It also, he says, addressed the concerns of sceptics:

> *There were a lot of people who I thought might not have initially seen the value, but they were thoughtfully engaged. If you present something that clearly articulates a compelling business case to people here, they are not going to stand in opposition to it.*

In the months leading up to the firm's partnership retreat, a working group of eight leaders developed the draft plan with the assistance of an outside adviser. An effective strategic plan does not need to be anything elaborate – for many outperforming firms it is a brass tacks outline of around five to eight pages setting out the vision and any needle-moving and measurable goals that are essential to achieving it.

At the retreat and in partner meetings leading up to it, Millard and the working group brought the entire partnership up to speed on the evolving competitive landscape by way of context; then Millard and the rest of the working group presented a working draft of the plan, demonstrating what it meant for the partnership.

> *I had a phrase that captured the aspiration – to lead at the intersection of alternative asset management, mergers and acquisitions and finance – and found myself repeating it so often I could hear it in my sleep.*

According to Millard, since the plan's implementation the firm's efforts have especially caught the attention of the top talent:

> *I think outperformers in particular take a lot of comfort in the fact that these plans were developed and successfully implemented.*

Simpson Thacher's experience shows that a firm in a strong position can effectively choose how it wants to be perceived and what it needs to prioritise for growth.

Of course, every strategic planning process presents challenges. One such challenge – ultimately an opportunity for Simpson Thacher's leadership – was to emphasise how achieving the firm's strategic priorities would benefit everyone in the firm, not just the partners in areas prioritised for growth. Put another way, a rising tide lifts all boats.

> *It was easier to talk about the sectors of focus. The message was that these areas are on track for outsized growth. But we expect growth and investment across the firm more broadly, too.*

The firm has achieved significant gains recently, particularly in areas prioritised for strategic growth. Throughout 2024 and 2025, the firm attracted numerous partners from other leading firms in areas including banking and credit, investment funds, M&A, energy and infrastructure, and executive compensation. These hires and others also strengthened capabilities in cities particularly targeted for outsized growth in the firm's plan, including New York and London.

While Simpson Thacher climbs toward achieving its plan, it continues to improve performance: for 2025 the firm reported around $3.5 billion in revenue and $8.57 million in profits per equity partner, according to Am Law data.[3]

Simpson Thacher's experience shows that a firm in a strong position can effectively choose how it wants to be perceived and what it needs to prioritise for growth. It can leverage its existing strengths in areas with increasing demand where the firm can command premium rates, driving significant growth in both revenue and profitability.

Takeaway: The process of developing a strategic plan helps partners align on their shared vision for the future of their practice. It clarifies what they want to achieve and establishes the measurable goals required to achieve it. It is easier for partners to do this when they have a clear understanding of their competitive landscape, how it is changing, and the potential costs of failing to make timely and effective strategic decisions.

3. Operationalising a plan

When Tim Mungovan was elected chair at Proskauer in January 2024, he made a clear statement to the firm's partners: that completing, operationalising and achieving a firm-wide strategic plan would be a top priority under his leadership. In addition to the firm as a whole, departments and practice groups would be required to develop their own plans – some for the first time. Some practice groups had articulated growth plans that their leaders reviewed and updated with frequency. Others had no plans at all.

While Proskauer had a solid foundation in many areas, the firm's ascent in recent years has been partly fuelled by its early entry market leadership in the world of private credit and private capital more generally. Its goal in mapping out a strategic plan was to build on its successes and prioritise the growth of practices adjacent and complementary to its strengths.

To begin the planning process, Mungovan asked an outside strategic adviser to address the partnership, to highlight the competitive threats in the marketplace and showcase how other firms had succeeded in executing on strategic plans. Mungovan then tasked each practice group with assembling practice-specific plans, and provided resources – such as a non-practising lawyer – to help partners develop those plans. He comments as follows:

> *I made clear to people what I believed were the foundations of the plan and what I was focused on, so that they could be focused on that, too ... The process of developing a firm-wide plan while also developing plans at the department and practice group level was somewhat unconventional but necessitated by a sense of urgency. I decided to refer to it as building the Intercontinental Railroad. We were going to race contemporaneously toward a median point.*

As with Alden Millard at Simpson Thacher, a significant part of Mungovan's work was gaining support from key partners whose support he knew he would need to build a broad consensus around the plan. After each practice group submitted its draft, he integrated the plans into a single document that captured a shared vision for the future, and a plan to achieve it. He then distilled scores of pages into a first draft of the plan, on which he sought input from key leaders in the firm, beginning with the managing partner (Ira Bogner) and prior chairs, as well as veteran partners and younger, high-performing and high-potential partners.

As a litigator at a firm that sought to build on its transactional strengths while deepening its litigation practice, Mungovan developed advocates for the plan by engaging with and listening carefully to a team of leaders across practices, ensuring broad support within the entire partnership. He and the managing partner had dozens of meetings over several months with partners – some in person, some by video, sometimes in groups and sometimes one-on-one. He made adjustments as needed to build consensus and gain support – while carefully preserving the core principles of the plan.

Mungovan then used a partner's meeting to present the plan to the entire partnership. He brought back the external adviser to clarify the competitive pressures Proskauer faced and would continue to face, absent change, which helped "deliver a lot of the tough messaging around what other really smart law firms were doing and how they were doing it", and paved the way for Mungovan to present the plan as a means for the firm to continue leveraging its strengths:

> *I set the profit and other goals, and explained how we were going to get there, with a focus on three or four key drivers that would power a steep rise.*

He notes the following:

> *[The drivers included] our culture, our willingness to collaborate, the fact that we are in great practices that have experienced great growth, and the fact that we are in the early stages of a time of significant transition using technology. And so, while other firms may be ahead of us today, they're not inevitably and irrevocably ahead of us. I used other firms as examples of competitors that outperformed over time and overtook their competition when nobody was really anticipating it. I used those examples to sort of communicate the idea of a path that we could lay out together, and the importance of that to our ability to control our own destiny.*

As Proskauer's experience demonstrates, working closely with leaders across practices and offices is often key to building consensus on and successfully executing a strategic plan, even when that plan prioritises a subset of practices for more aggressive near-term growth.

The firm has now shifted to the execution stage:

> *Now the key is in allocating profits, making sure that we're doing it through the lens of the strategic plan. We're executing using the strategic plan and making our decisions around laterals to prioritize time and money around investments that extend existing strengths and make the firm more dominant in areas such as private capital, which causes a tide to rise to the benefit of all practices and people in the firm.*

Proskauer has already achieved success since executing the plan. The firm reported an increase in gross revenue in 2025 over the previous year of 13.8%, to $1.58 billion, and profits per equity partner rose by nearly 12.6% to cross the $5 million mark ($5.02 million). The firm has had a non-equity tier for almost 20 years.

Proskauer has continued to build on its hiring goals with several lateral additions in key markets such as London and in private credit and adjacent practices. Recent hires include: four finance partners from Cadwalader, Wickersham & Taft that led the firm to open in Charlotte; private equity partner Sarah Stasny from Paul Weiss to lead the firm's private equity transactional practice; two lawyers from A&O Shearman in London, including Philip Bowden, the firm's head of private capital; and an eight-partner fund formation group in Paris from Simmons & Simmons, as well as a three-partner group from Hogan Lovells' Paris office in February 2026.

Takeaway: As Proskauer's experience demonstrates, working closely with leaders across practices and offices is often key to building consensus on and successfully executing a strategic plan, even when that plan prioritises a subset of practices for more aggressive near-term growth.

Notes

1 See Susan Beck, "Big Law and Legal Aid", *The American Lawyer*, July 2015, www.lsc.gov/sites/default/files/LSC/pdfs/AmericanLawyer-JusticeGap.pdf.

2 ALM, Law.com Compass, "Simpson Thacher", www.law.com/compass/firm/LF00001071/Simpson-Thacher/overview.

3 Patrick Smith, "Simpson's Revenue and Profits Surge, Amid Rapid Partnership Expansion", Law.com, 6 April 2026, www.law.com/americanlawyer/2026/04/06/simpsons-revenue-and-profits-surge-amid-rapid-partnership-expansion/.

IV. Compensation as strategic accelerator

1. Introduction

In today's highly competitive market for top-performing partners, especially those who are significant contributors or rising stars, firms are encountering unprecedented challenges in their efforts to attract and retain talent. As they navigate these challenges, one of the most difficult strategic decisions firms face is how to adapt their approach to partner compensation to a dynamic and ever-changing landscape.

Outperforming firms are competing for a relatively small pool of coveted lawyers, and, at the top of the market, they are sometimes offering compensation packages that reach above $30 million annually to lure them and keep them.

Attracting and retaining significant contributors is widely perceived as both the biggest opportunity and the biggest threat facing high-performing firms today. Or as Brad Karp, who chaired Paul Weiss from 2008 to 2026, puts it:

> *The foundational point would be, at the end of the day, firms like ours are in the talent business, and there is a tremendous competitive push to attract and retain as many stars as you can possibly have.*

Firms that have been successful in attracting and retaining sought-after talent in this environment have demonstrated key characteristics including flexibility to meet and often exceed the market on compensation, starting at the top. A drive to change, to be as competitive as possible, can take different forms.

Outperforming firms have often taken steps including revisiting and, in most cases, modifying or abandoning rigid structures such as lockstep in favour of more flexible, merit-driven approaches. They increasingly use bonuses for extraordinary performance and prioritise redistributing their net income from lower-performing partners in lower compensation deciles to higher-performing partners in higher deciles, particularly those the firm can least afford to lose, such as outsized contributors and the next generation of them.

To do this, many high-performing firms, by definition, reduce compensation for partners who have benefited from the firm's profitability without improving their own performance, in favour of rewarding those whose contributions have grown materially and moved the needle for the firm.

Beyond that, outperforming firms are not just reallocating; they are putting themselves in a position to have more to allocate by aggressively increasing their profitability and often their scale. All the while, firms have made these changes while balancing the need to compete with peers on size, profitability, quality, culture and market leadership, a balance that is typically challenging given competing priorities.

Figure 1: Increasing PPEP by Am Law 100 gross revenue segment

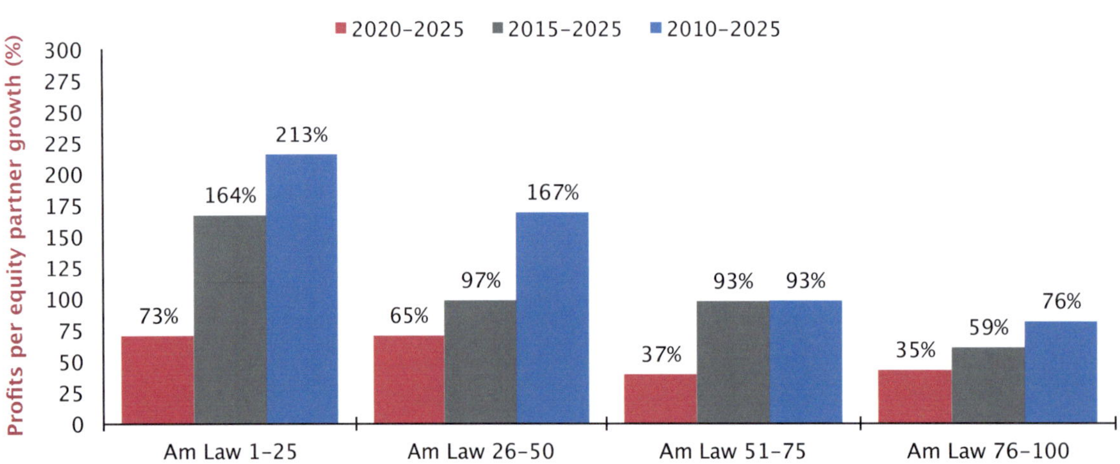

In this chapter, we focus on several firms, including Paul Weiss and Davis Polk, that are navigating these changes and positioning themselves to gain advantages relative to the pack in the competition for talent.

While these two firms differ from one another and from most others in the market, the competitive forces at play operate in generally the same way across all firms at the conceptual level. Everything is relative.

2. Changing old approaches

By the dawn of the millennium, New York firms were no longer just competing against themselves for talent. Instead, they found themselves confronted by a small group of competitors that were becoming larger and more profitable – firms with roots in other markets.

Among initially rising competitors to Wall Street firms, some have since become considerably larger and among the most profitable. Firms like Kirkland & Ellis and Latham & Watkins have increased their flexibility on compensation relative to competitors by leveraging their scale and strong profitability. They capitalise on the weaknesses

Change from the outside ... triggered change inside some of the industry's most exclusive and venerated firms.

of certain competitors, particularly those with less scale and a less established culture of meritocracy in compensation and advancement. For the smaller and less meritocratic firms, this can hinder the ability to attract and retain top and rising star talent, especially rising stars in their 30s and 40s who often earn below – and sometimes far below – what they could command in the open market.

Change from the outside, in other words, triggered change inside some of the industry's most exclusive and venerated firms. The change initially took the form of altering the traditional approach to lockstep to allow for more flexibility at the top to retain and attract particularly significant contributors. But in some firms, change has more recently gone much further. As Brad Karp explains:

> *From both a defensive and a competitive strategic perspective, we returned the volley and other firms, because we did it, began to say, "You know what, we're going to have to loosen up our pay structure too." You fast forward to now, and most of the elite Wall Street firms are paying their top partners well above the traditional lockstep.*

Historically, Paul Weiss had regularly ranked in the top 10 firms by profits per equity partner and it still does, according to *American Lawyer* rankings. It had and still has a highly sought-after list of institutional clients. While it routinely hired lateral partners, the compensation it offered to laterals was frequently in line with compensation for similarly performing homegrown partners in the firm.

But the financial crisis that began in 2008 drove change. Paul Weiss, like some other large and diversified firms, had relied in part on its litigation practice to power it through tough years triggered by the financial crisis. Karp, himself a litigator, recalls:

> *We had a dominant litigation and white-collar practice. We did not have dominant transactional practices. The transactional markets had seized up, and the litigation practices, especially white collar representing the banks, were incredibly busy. We were doing comparatively extraordinarily well in the marketplace. So, we had a lot of capital.*

When the financial crisis ebbed, Karp observed the emergence of new dynamics for talent and business generation, ones that focused more on transactional work:

> *I thought it was really important for us to invest. Looking at the firm, which was largely a New York-centric firm at that point, it was really important to invest in transactional talent.*

Karp was responding to the trends he witnessed in the marketplace, such as firms boosting their market share in alternative and rapidly growing asset classes like private equity, private credit and other innovative forms of private capital investment and finance.

One firm that was on a sharp ascent coming out of the global financial crisis, Kirkland, became the poster child of firms that were benefiting from the rise of private equity. As it increased its scale and profitability from its early market leadership in private equity, benefiting initially from a sizeable portfolio of fund clients from outside of the bulge bracket, Kirkland drew on its war chest to make its mark in New York by hiring lateral partners with attention-grabbing compensation packages from firms that rarely lost partners to rivals.

Most had not focused on private equity as much as Kirkland had from the early innings, and some still had an approach to compensation heavily influenced by lockstep at the time, making it relatively straightforward for Kirkland to exploit a below-market ceiling on compensation at those firms for mid-career rising stars. At the time, relatively early in its New York build, Kirkland looked like an emerging prize fighter taking on soon-to-be former world champs who had one hand tied behind their back.

In this context, Kirkland developed a frequent pattern of poaching 30–40-year-old rising stars with extensive runway in their careers from firms that paid them below what their performance merited on the market because of their lack of seniority relative to more senior high-performing partners in the firm. For this reason, some Wall Street firms became highly exposed to losing their outsized contributors and their rising stars.

As Karp recalls: "Kirkland began to circle our partners and offer them very large pay packages."

And so Karp wanted to both act defensively to retain the firm's existing top talent and burnish its own transactional practice. The firm did this by building out its own depth of quality and position of market leadership in the practices that were fuelling the rapidly growing money practices.

One way Karp bolstered Paul Weiss's transactional practices was by deepening its relationship with asset management firm Apollo Global Management. As it beefed up its lateral hiring, the firm made a splash by attracting a transactional team from O'Melveny & Myers in 2011, including corporate finance partner Gregory Ezring and tax partner Brad Okun, who had both served in leadership roles at O'Melveny. Many see that as an important turning point for Paul Weiss toward the firm that it is today.

As the competition for transactional work intensified, work for alternative asset classes continued to command premium billing rates. This was unsurprising given the demand for the best lawyers in this area and the relatively limited supply of them, coupled with the value the firms helped their clients to create.

It is widely believed in the market that Paul Weiss leveraged its relationship with Apollo, following valuable litigation wins for the fund, to attract the O'Melveny partners on whom the fund was relying for important portions of its transactional work. This turned out to be a very strategic move that many firms have replicated, by leaning on their clients to identify and attract lateral partners from other firms, in their efforts to entice highly sought-after teams in competitive practices and cities.

As the competition for transactional work intensified, work for alternative asset classes continued to command premium billing rates. This was unsurprising given the demand for the best lawyers in this area and the relatively limited supply of them, coupled with the value the firms helped their clients to create.

Karp knew that for Paul Weiss to develop a bigger and more dominant transactional practice, he needed to make blockbuster hires. To meet this goal, the firm would need to make large investments, which would require evolving and increasing the flexibility of the firm's approach to compensation, particularly at the top. He explains:

> *At that moment, having a fiduciary duty to the firm and to my partnership, we had to come up with a solution that did not cost us our important talent. So, we decided that we were going to increase the top end of our scale, keeping about 85% of our partners in the traditional lockstep, but at the very top end, pay bonuses.*

By breaking lockstep, Karp put the firm in a position to pay the top 15% highest compensated partners above, or in some cases well above, the rest of the partnership.

A modified lockstep model proved crucial, serving as a bridge to a longer-term solution for successfully competing with peers that compensate on merit. Like many of its peers, Paul Weiss's approach is now more of a sky-is-the-limit approach to compensating its outsized contributors, increasing the firm's flexibility to retain them and attract more. As Karp says:

> *Eight to 10 years ago is when it first really started for us. It was okay, because the bonuses were paid to a relatively small number of partners, and they were paid to a very obvious number of partners. The partnership at large would look at all of our pay as transparent. We'll look into who is receiving the extra bonuses. [The partnership said] okay, that makes perfect sense. That person has a very, very significant practice. I'm comfortable with that.*

These changes preceded a blockbuster addition to the firm. In 2016, Paul Weiss attracted prominent M&A partner Scott Barshay from Cravath, Swaine & Moore, then a lockstep firm, giving Barshay, according to Karp, a "material pay increase" over his compensation at Cravath. Fast-forward, and Barshay became the chair of the corporate practice at Paul Weiss and more recently chair of the firm, succeeding Karp.[1]

Karp says the financial crisis, in addition to driving Paul Weiss's decision to prioritise growth of its transactional practice, also destabilised the client/firm relationship dynamic in favour of individual attorneys rather than the firms they worked for, thus driving greater 'star' influence in the market:

> *[Prior to the financial crisis] you could pretty much go through the Fortune 50 and tell what their main law firm was. That began to break apart during the financial crisis, and that has completely broken apart over the last decade.*

While not common at that time, ten-figure compensation packages are now increasingly common for top performers at certain outperforming firms, particularly within certain highly profitable transactional practices.

There has been some compensation inflation as $10 million pay packages have become $15 million packages, then $20 million packages and, for a small number of partners, packages in the $30 million range and above. It's likely the trend will continue among the highest performers, particularly in the largest and most profitable firms. This trend coincides with others, including the rise of private equity and other forms of private capital and finance, and the rise of law firm billing rates that have reached $3,000 an hour and will very likely surpass $5,000 an hour before long.

Blockbuster hires like Barshay and others who are less well known have become increasingly common, and firms make such investments to stay competitive with outperforming rivals. Firms in the top 20 ranked by profitability, and some in other parts of the market, sometimes offer coveted partners as much as two to three times the partner's current compensation to entice them to move.

Karp sees the changes that Paul Weiss has made as part of a movement within a cohort of outperforming firms:

> *Most of the firms have loosened the compensation parameters such that the top partners, who are perceived to be the most productive partners, are paid bonuses that put them above the*

rank-and-file partners in the partnership. That's where we are. I cannot conceive of a braking mechanism that's going to stop this trend.

As Paul Weiss's experience shows, the market for talent is open, and being competitive with peer firms – whatever the practice or geography – requires being able to be competitive on, or at least in the same league on, compensation and compensation potential for stars and rising stars.

As with most goods, the price of talent varies with supply and demand over time. More firms are seeking ways to free up capital to incentivise high-performing contributors to join or remain on their platforms, and firms in the Am Law 20 and the Am Law 200 alike find themselves steeped in this rapidly escalating war for talent.

However, not all firms have the same firepower in this competition. Benchmarking data that we have collected from a sample of approximately half of the Am Law 100 evidences a growing trend: larger and more profitable firms compensate more on average than other firms, at the top of the top decile of partners, at the bottom of the top decile of partners, and even among new equity partners. This often gives them a talent advantage, which often translates into advantages in the competition for desirable clients and work.

We would emphasise that this trend does not exist only at the top of the market. Rather, the same forces operate across all firms, regardless of profile, relative to their competitive set. Movement at the top of the market often dominoes throughout the market more broadly.

Takeaway: Addressing obstacles to flexibility in compensation is crucial. This includes paying top performers based on merit, ensuring that compensation is competitive in the market, and to get there often using meaningful bonuses strategically. Allocating more distributable net income to partners who are essential to the firm's success is a frequent part of the calculus annually in many high-performing firms.

At the same time, increasing profitability and scaling revenues are viewed as essential in most firms striving to get to the next level to improve their performance and market position. All these factors typically create a competitive advantage in attracting talent, which can lead to additional benefits such as a stronger brand, better client relationships and greater success in competing for particularly desirable mandates.

3. The cultural element

When firms decide to evolve their approach to compensation, often with an eye toward aligning their approach with what it will take to achieve the firm's strategy, they can face a balancing act in introducing more flexibility while preserving important aspects of the firm's culture. This was the challenge Neil Barr faced when he began transitioning Davis Polk, which had historically had a traditional lockstep system, to a hybrid system in 2019.

Davis Polk's roots date back more than 150 years, and as a new chair who had just taken the reins of the firm, Barr worked diligently to address the firm's cultural elements as he convinced the partnership of the necessity of a major shift in its approach to compensation:

> *I think, in a firm like ours, there was a fallacy that needed to be rebutted, which is that compensation and culture are synonymous. They're not. But I think lockstep firms tell themselves that lockstep is a culture. It's not. It's a seniority-based compensation system that has good things about it and bad things about it, and it's an anachronistic structure as well. I worked with my partners through the proposition that there were parts of our culture that were exceptional, and there were parts that were not right.*

Faced with the same threat of increasing competition for the firm's talent that other New York-centric firms were facing, Barr was one of many chairs of outperforming New York firms who came to the conclusion that the firm was potentially vulnerable to losing key partners and would face challenges in growing if it retained its lockstep compensation structure. Barr says:

> *We ultimately decided that we could not compete in the market and grow the firm as we needed to as a pure lockstep firm. We recognized that there was going to be a little bit of an evolution in our compensation philosophy.*

Barr's goal, in essence, was not to introduce a wholesale transformation of the firm's compensation model. Rather, he wanted to create an understanding in the partnership that a modification to the structure, while potentially challenging, was both advantageous and necessary for the firm to successfully compete in an evolving and increasingly competitive market for talent:

> *I spoke to every single partner, one on one, we had focus groups, we did a lot of consultation in our partnership. The first thing we did was articulate our firm's core values. Who are we, what is it that we aspire to do, and what should our compensation system achieve? And we actually aligned our partnership around that*

sort of architecture before we went into any model development of what the right system was.

Barr centred discussions of the firm's existing ethos in his pitch for change:

We still wanted to be a law firm that trades most significantly in the excellence of our lawyers and our client outcomes. We wanted to be a law firm that has a team-oriented culture and the least amount of friction possible in getting to the best client answer. We want this to be a satisfying professional home for folks. We wanted to be explicit in that. We went through an exercise. We had an outside advisor interview all of our partners as well. It was a very significant exercise. We formed an advisory board of partners to be a sounding board for various things that we were doing.

As the firm went through the details of changing its structure, including financial modelling and an evangelising campaign to the partnership, Barr emphasised transparent and consistent communication, especially on the notion of comparative compensation, or compensation as it relates directly to what an attorney could make at a firm of similar stature:

Introducing the concept of comparative compensation in our firm was really hard and required a lot of hyper-communication within the firm around what we were valuing. But, fundamentally, I think [it boiled down to] getting folks comfortable with the proposition that we could continue to be Davis Polk but do it in a different way. That was really the hard part.

Davis Polk's modified lockstep system provided specific compensation enhancements for partners based on their contributions to client- and firm-centred work. Yet the firm did not want rapid, radical change, and it decided not to implement certain changes that were commonplace at other firms at that time, such as bonuses. As Barr explains:

We don't do any form of bonuses. The unit allocations are pre-agreed. So for us, that makes a lot of sense, we don't reward a good year or dock people for a bad year, because it's to an extent progressive and seniority-oriented.

Barr's approach to developing, building consensus around and implementing a new approach to compensation aligns with many of the successful strategies for building broad consensus in the context of strategic planning discussed in Chapter III, "The value of a strategic plan". Barr convened small-group and full-partner meetings. While pay increases at the top end of the pay scale are the focus of many firms' recent compensation changes, Barr saw an opportunity to retain up-and-coming talent by strengthening the financial position of those in the middle of the compensation bell curve. He explains:

> *One of the design choices we made in 2020 was actually to get more money to our mid-level partners faster. Our senior partners and our highest performers were cognizant of the need to protect that class. A number of our senior partners said that "I think the right thing for this firm is to shore up the next generation". And so there was a lot of consultation with the next generation as well.*

He continues:

> *That consultation also extended to specific issues, such as family leave and gender diversity, as a non-lockstep model actually had the opportunity to complicate matters.*

Takeaway: Moving towards a new approach to compensation can and usually does require an exercise in consensus building, which can mean listening to and eventually evangelising partner by partner, with a focus on high-performing individuals, to identify and address concerns, questions and other input from given groups of the partnership.

In some cases, as firms evolve their approach to compensation, they also revisit which parts of their culture are most important to protect.

4. Grappling with transparency

Transparency is a significant cultural issue that many firms grapple with, particularly as they evolve their approach to compensation. Firms often benefit from determining the threshold of transparency they are comfortable with within the bounds of their culture, while balancing this against what will be necessary to attract and retain impactful partners to succeed in the competition for desirable clients and work.

In some cases, as firms evolve their approach to compensation, they also revisit which parts of their culture are most important to protect. Those who find that a culture of excellence is indispensable to achieving their aspirations sometimes make a strategic choice to be less transparent. This puts the firm in a more flexible position to keep up with the rising market for compensation to retain and attract the people the firm will need to live up to its commitment to consistent excellence.

However, many firms feel they have no choice but to maintain the transparency of their system. Some have undermined their competitiveness as a result of that decision. Others choose to adopt a less transparent approach over time to foster harmony among disparately compensated partners.

Some firms find a middle ground, such as maintaining a closed system during the early years of a partner's career or taking other smaller steps to reduce the public visibility of compensation, such as making the compensation of all partners available only to other partners within the confines of a chair's office.

Still other firms, rather than releasing individual compensation and metrics, release compensation bands to provide partners with relative information, but not information with which they can make apples-to-apples comparisons with other individuals, which is the most frequent source of dissatisfaction, appeals, and sometimes departures.

In Paul Weiss's case, bringing in laterals at higher levels of compensation relative to similarly performing homegrown partners sparked an internal conversation about balancing transparency with efforts to retain high-performing partners and attract others seen as necessary to achieve the partnership's aspirations and remain top of market. Karp notes:

> *If you're taking a lateral, you almost always have to pay a premium to get them. They're leaving their existing platform, and you have to make it worth their while. They're going through a lot of tumult to switch firms and deal with client transitions. What would happen if you take a lateral and the lateral would get more money than the*

As firms adapt their compensation strategies to tackle the growing competition for talent, they can benefit from aligning their approach to compensation with accelerating the achievement of their strategic goals, all while preserving the most positive aspects of their culture.

> *existing partner. You wind up making an incredibly valued and valuable existing partner who has done everything right feel like a second-class citizen when the sheet [showing partner compensation] comes around once a year, and it says 'Charlie' [the lateral in this example] is getting $8.5 million and 'Jane' [the established partner] is getting $6.5 million when 'Charlie' and 'Jane' have essentially the same practice.*

He continues:

> *You're creating these distinctions and demarcations that are very difficult to swallow, challenging to justify. I really do believe that, in valuing and respecting our partners, and I hated signaling to the firm that someone is an A+ partner based on the compensation and another person who's just as good and just as valuable is a B+ partner, because there's a compensation differential that can't be justified under ordinary metrics.*

Paul Weiss's solution was to move the firm to a so-called 'black box' compensation model – one that does not offer transparency within the partnership about each partner's compensation. The change wasn't something that Karp arrived at lightly or rapidly. He recalls:

In the two years before we announced it, I started to lay the groundwork for the idea, saying in my speeches, our system doesn't really accommodate the competitive realities of the compensation marketplace today, and we should actually think about going to a black box or closed system.

While challenging, Karp says the timing of the change was also crucial to its internal approval and acceptance.

We moved to a black box system during a time when we had an extraordinarily profitable year, and all 180 of our partners saw their compensation increase under the black box, so no one looked at their number and said, "Oh my god, I can't believe they did that to me." Good timing.

I think they trusted that I would make fair decisions or that our comp system under me would make fair decisions.

Nevertheless, not every high-performing firm has chosen to abandon transparency in its compensation practices, and for good reason. In fact, most firms with an open approach to compensation have difficulty envisioning adopting a closed compensation approach within the bounds of their culture.

Barr, for example, saw a black box system as a bridge too far at Davis Polk and elected to maintain a transparent system. In doing so, Barr says he assessed both the firm's tolerance for an opaque model and his ability, as a younger new chair, to realistically shepherd such a change through the firm at that point in his tenure. "I think the very first question that I was asked when we decided to change was, 'Is it going to be transparent?'" he says, referring to black box models at other firms.

Takeaway: As firms adapt their compensation strategies to tackle the growing competition for talent, they can benefit from aligning their approach to compensation with accelerating the achievement of their strategic goals, all while preserving the most positive aspects of their culture.

Note

1 Scott Barshay was appointed chair of Paul Weiss in February 2026, succeeding Brad Karp.

Effective investment in laterals and groups has become a very important (if not the most important) ingredient in the success of most outperforming firms. It is widely seen as necessary and the only way, short of M&A, to remain competitive with or ahead of rivals on size, profitability and depth of quality in areas that often drive perception of market leadership.

V. Lateral hires and teams: accelerating the strategy

1. Introduction

Strategic growth and investment in laterals and groups have picked up considerably in recent years. As we've discussed, this aligns with the strategic imperative that most firms have to accelerate the pace at which they simultaneously grow scale, profitability and market leadership in chosen areas.

Effective investment in laterals and groups has become a very important (if not the most important) ingredient in the success of most outperforming firms. It is widely seen as necessary and the only way, short of M&A, to remain competitive with or ahead of rivals on size, profitability and depth of quality in areas that often drive perception of market leadership.

A variety of changing dynamics paved the way for the hyper-competitive market for talent that presently exists, including the fact that larger and more profitable firms within a competitive set tend to have greater flexibility on compensation. That reality, coupled with the shift by most high-performing firms to a meritocratic approach to partner compensation, has made it much easier than it used to be for a high-performing partner to substantially increase their compensation by merely changing firms.

The amount of money at stake is also a factor driving more frequent moves. A 'star' class of high-impact, highly compensated partners has emerged within a small group of firms, with a recent sharp rise in the number of partners compensated in the eight-figure range. Even for laterals outside that range, recruiters and firms often communicate directly about their potential earning power and runway at specific firms versus others, which also drives greater movement and advantages for firms with higher compensation ceilings.

In a nutshell, differentials among rival firms have grown in terms of size, profitability and flexibility in compensation. As this has happened, larger and more profitable firms have come to pay more than others on average. Concurrently, there has been a sharp increase in the movement of laterals and groups between firms.

For all of these reasons, most outperforming firms have accepted that lateral hiring is the primary way to achieve the benefits of scale while continuing to enhance profitability and market leadership. Most have concluded that it will be very difficult, if not impossible, to grow key performance metrics important to them at a market-competitive pace through organic, up-through-the-ranks growth alone. Some of those firms increasingly feel they may need to put M&A on the table because there are limits on how much they can scale with laterals net of retirements and other departures.

The success rate that firm leaders perceive for their lateral hires varies. Generally, it is lower than most firms would prefer. Over the years, many chairs have mentioned to us privately that they are satisfied with about one-third of the lateral hires they made 18 months earlier. The likelihood of success in lateral hiring tends to increase when firms hire groups rather than individuals. Additionally, success rates improve when laterals or groups are identified and recommended by key clients or high-performing partners within the firm.

In this chapter, we delve into the strategies for lateral hiring that several outperforming firms have developed and executed on successfully to accelerate the achievement of their strategy. As part of that, we will explore the varied experiences of firms such as Kirkland & Ellis, Orrick, Herrington & Sutcliffe, Proskauer Rose, Sidley Austin and Wachtell, Lipton, Rosen & Katz to show how different firms effectively compete for talent and build their firms for the future.

2. Active approaches

For Mitch Zuklie, chair of Orrick, a key to hiring is determining whether a potential hire will fit Orrick's culture and growth goals. Zuklie's methodology in the hiring process centres on always asking a probing

[M]ost outperforming firms have accepted that lateral hiring is the primary way to achieve the benefits of scale while continuing to enhance profitability and market leadership.

question of the potential candidate – one whose answer will help to reveal whether the candidate will fit in:

> *When I talk to laterals, the one question I ask every time is: How do you define success in three years? How will you measure success for you, for your team, for your family? What support do you think you need from us to achieve that? And if someone can't answer that question, we'll never hire them. Ever. If that's not part of the way they're thinking about the world and they haven't thought that through, there's no way they're going to fit on our platform.*

The idea behind this question, Zuklie explains, is to screen potential laterals to understand both how they will contribute to the firm and how the firm can enhance that partner's practice. If the relationship is not reciprocal, the match is unlikely to succeed.

There are other arrows in the quiver of firms that have dominated the lateral market. For example, Kirkland & Ellis lawyers, working with business development professionals, maintain a targeted list of partners and groups the firm would like to attract in order to grow out specific practice areas and important client relationships. Knowing that some of these potential hires can take years to come to fruition, Kirkland lawyers regularly check in with these potential laterals to gauge interest in joining the firm and stay on their radar.

Kirkland is also disciplined about regularly consulting with strategically important clients on who the firm should hire to strengthen and grow the relationship.

Consultations with clients also often helps the firm identify areas where it has capability gaps in the minds of important clients. Kirkland lawyers will identify key clients with whom to have open conversations about the lawyers they rely on at other firms. These conversations, in turn, inform the firm's hiring strategy. Kirkland will make the pitch that it would like to handle more work for the client. The client, in turn, will tell Kirkland about partners at other firms that handle that work. As Kirkland chair Jon Ballis explains:

> *Every now and then, a big client will come to us. They'll say, "We'd love to work more with Kirkland. We love your culture and how you do business. But you know, our GC has worked with this lawyer, this team of lawyers at this firm. So if you go hire that person, that would be really good for us." So we'll sometimes do that too.*

Takeaway: Outperforming firms take dogged and highly strategic approaches to luring laterals, often focusing on those who their clients know and value.

3. A different approach

Andrew Nussbaum and Bill Savitt, the co-chairs of Wachtell, lead a firm that is something of an anomaly in the Am Law 100. The firm is much smaller than its closest rivals ($1.39 billion in revenue in 2025, brought in by a partnership of 79, according to Am Law). But Wachtell occupies a distinctive position among law firms, which enables it to consistently rank among the most profitable in the world, with profits per equity partner exceeding $12 million in 2025, according to Am Law.

In addition to being distinctive for its smaller size and higher profitability relative to most competitors, Wachtell is one of the few firms that still maintains a lockstep approach to partner compensation, rarely pursues lateral partners, and does not have a non-equity partner tier: "We are not active in the lateral partner market," Nussbaum says. "It's very rare."

Nussbaum says that the firm, even in today's dynamic hiring market, is better served by developing its talent organically, meaning bringing lawyers up through its ranks and promoting from within most of the time:

> *We do think a lot about what makes this place work, and it is the fact that people who work with each other, not necessarily that they're your best friend, but that they're people you really like*

working with; therefore, the best way to experience that is to start with attorneys when they are relatively young and to build them. That's a rewarding part of the practice, actually, as a partner. We have some corporate attorneys here who are in their early 40s and responsible for some of our most important matters and largest fees. That's possible because we all work together, and we embrace each other's success.

While Wachtell has thrived on lockstep and at a smaller scale relative to its closest competitors, that approach is challenging for most firms that are less profitable. Wachtell also benefits from its reputation as a dominant market leader in the relatively narrow and premium rate areas on which its practice focuses, which has given it a significant competitive advantage.

4. Team hiring

Outperforming firms are increasingly acting on the strategic imperative to strengthen and grow their best client relationships by hiring sought-after partners and teams in areas for which the firm wants to be known and that their clients value. Ballis calls this practice 'talent aggregation'.

"We are not active in the lateral partner market. It's very rare."

Andrew Nussbaum, co-chair, Wachtell, Lipton, Rosen & Katz

In January 2025, for example, Kirkland hired a team of five partners from Skadden, Arps, Slate, Meagher & Flom, helmed by partner Alli Brown in Philadelphia. Brown is a pre-eminent trial lawyer known for a nationally recognised pharmaceutical and medical products liability practice and has earned numerous honours over the years, including being named a Litigator of the Year by *The American Lawyer.*

"She's the best of the best," Ballis says of Brown. "We have massive demand. We don't have enough players to handle it." Shortly after hiring the Skadden team, Kirkland also hired a group of approximately 30 mass tort lawyers from King & Spalding.

Firms lower in the market, with smaller scale and lower profitability, can rarely make back-to-back investments of size in highly profitable practices. By contrast, Kirkland benefits from a very large net income pool, made possible by its scale and profitability advantages relative to competitors, resulting in each investment, even if considered large for most firms, representing a materially smaller percentage of income.

This reduces partners' concern about making significant investments on a regular basis. Leaders of firms with much greater scale and net income tend to receive far less pushback from their partners about making large investments.

"We never hire someone because of their book of business. Ever. We hire people because we think they're super-talented."

Jon Ballis, chair, Kirkland & Ellis

Interestingly, Kirkland's goal is often not to simply hire a group that brings a book of business. In fact, in many cases, Kirkland is not concerned if a lateral partner brings their clients to the firm. As Ballis explains:

> *We never hire someone because of their book of business. Ever. We hire people because we think they're super-talented.*

The long-term goal of bringing on prized lateral groups, often identified by important clients, says Ballis, is to support the firm's existing clients and to grow and strengthen these relationships for the long term:

> *We are able to make the arrows go both ways. We're able to leverage their skill set into our client base or potential client base, which makes their practice better, and they are able to leverage our platform with the skills and the talent we have throughout our network to make their practice better.*

Group hiring has also been transformative for Sidley. One of the firm's strategic priorities in recent years has been the expansion of sophisticated transactional areas, including private equity, M&A and finance. A transformative moment for the firm came in 2015 when the then-chair of the firm's management committee, Larry Barden, led an effort to prioritise the growth of a large private equity practice that some of the firm's rivals had focused on building for years, but Sidley had not prioritised as much before Barden's tenure.

Part of Barden's approach was to hire not only excellent lawyers and business developers but also people committed to building the practice – including excellent recruiters and potential future leaders dedicated to building something larger than themselves. That approach led to a critical inflection point in 2015 with the hire of Dan Clivner from Simpson Thacher, followed by a series of other impactful hires, resulting in a team that together built a leading international private equity practice.

Clivner would later become global co-chair of M&A and private equity, alongside Brian Fahrney, who would later become chair of Sidley's executive committee. Together, they hired Mehdi Khodadad and a team from Cooley in 2019. Khodadad had such a significant impact on Sidley's rise in private equity and M&A that, about six years after his start at the firm, he became the global leader of its M&A and private equity practice, and more recently became a member of the firm's nine-member management committee.

Sidley has a history of elevating lateral partners into important leadership roles. For example, Yvette Ostolaza joined the firm from Weil, Gotshal & Manges in 2013, where she served on Weil's management committee and co-led the commercial litigation group. At Sidley, she led the firm's global litigation practice and served on the executive committee before becoming chair of the management committee in 2022. During Ostolaza's term, Sidley has attracted leaders in several high-profile practices, including private equity, real estate, restructuring, global finance and product liability litigation.

More recently, consistent with market trends, Sidley has made a series of key hires in New York through single and small-group additions, including M&A partners from Latham, Paul Weiss, Jones Day, Cravath, Simpson Thacher, and a trio of private equity lawyers from Fried, Frank, Harris, Shriver & Jacobson in late 2024.

By 2025, New York would become Sidley's largest office, capping a long history in the market that accelerated in 2001 when the firm acquired Wall Street firm Brown & Wood. Hiring there continued in the spring of 2025 when the firm brought on a sizeable finance team from Cadwalader, Wickersham & Taft, including Bonnie Neuman, a management committee member and practice chair at her former firm. Yvette Ostolaza explains:

> *We have focused on consolidating clients on our global platform by approaching teams who already serve our clients. It is a winning strategy that makes for a seamless transition to our platform.*

A common thread among outperforming firms is that New York has been their highest priority for strategic growth for decades. This stands to reason, given that law has generally been a follow-the-money profession and New York is the largest and most prosperous city in the United States, in addition to being the world's top financial centre. The city has more premium talent and work that commands premium rates for law firms than any other city in the world.

After New York, an additional high-priority city for Sidley and many other high-performing firms is London, the second-largest financial centre
in the world. Sidley opened in London in 1974 and, like many high-performing firms, has accelerated its growth there in recent years. The firm recruited at least 10 partners from Latham & Watkins in London in 2024 and 2025, including teams focused on leveraged finance.

As Sidley co-chair Brian Fahrney explains:

> *It's just about being relentless and going after the right people. You're bringing new clients on board, but you're also hiring people*

who can help you build the next level and the next level and the next level. The amount of investment is significant, and you have to have the balance sheet to do it and the will to stay committed to the approach. You have to have the will to invest in certain places that others might not be able to or have the will to do so.

Takeaway: Group hires are an impactful driver of growth for many outperforming firms because, when carefully and strategically selected, they add more than just headcount; they can also transform a firm's practice, bringing about exponential change more rapidly than one-off hires. Firms with more scale and profitability in a competitive set tend to have more flexibility to recruit and retain needle-moving groups more often.

5. Star hires

Another approach to lateral hiring that has helped many outperforming firms fuel revenue and profitability growth is the strategic hiring of transformative stars. This approach is typically contingent on the ability to offer large, competitive compensation packages that can attract a star partner from their current firm.

Kirkland has embraced this approach and, over the years, has made a series of transformational hires. Examples include litigator Sandra

Group hires are an impactful driver of growth for many outperforming firms because, when carefully and strategically selected, they add more than just headcount; they can also transform a firm's practice, bringing about exponential change more rapidly than one-off hires.

Goldstein, hired from Cravath in 2018, and corporate lawyer Andrew Calder from Simpson Thacher in 2014. Calder has helped lead the growth of Kirkland's Texas-focused practice to more than 500 lawyers and more than $1 billion in revenue in less than 10 years.

Brad Karp of Paul Weiss attributes the trend of star partner hiring in part to changes in the relationships between institutional clients and their outside counsel. Traditionally, large institutions such as banks and blue-chip companies maintained seemingly unbreakable ties to specific law firms, relying on them for a substantial share of the sophisticated legal work they outsourced.

That is not necessarily the case any longer, and the shift has caused disruptions, as mentioned in Chapter IV, "Compensation as strategic accelerator".

These institutional changes were among the factors that prompted Karp's decision to hire star transactional partner Scott Barshay from Cravath in 2016. Karp referred to Barshay as a 'unicorn' who could help the firm advance its transactional practice. Barshay's addition enabled Paul Weiss to attract other transactional leaders to the firm, including, more recently, a group of 13 corporate partners from Kirkland in September 2023. This team contributed to growing the firm's public and private transactional practice and expanding its presence in challenging markets such as London.

Paul Weiss had 34 attorneys in its London office in 2023. Today, it has over 200. As Karp explains:

> *The market for star partners is very hot. Star partners can command enhanced compensation because clients follow them, and the revenues follow them. There's a demand for them. Stars beget stars. They want to go to a place where they can look and say, "There are other star partners already there. They know how to accommodate stars. I'd like to be part of that platform."*

Takeaway: Star partners are often not only excellent at doing the work and bringing it in, but are also often builders with a network effect. The most valuable star partners often make outsized contributions in bringing in and growing important client relationships, raising the firm's profile and enhancing its brand, and helping to recruit other stars, rising stars and desirable teams. They are sometimes seen as potential future leaders of the firm, and contributors. The best also add to the strength of the glue that binds partners together.

6. Looking to the strategic plan

Bureaucratic red tape, including the requirement of multiple committee approvals to bring on new laterals, can present hurdles to strategic growth. Firms that agree on their growth goals in advance can smooth the path to move the needle more quickly.

For Proskauer, for example, whose approach to strategic planning we discussed in Chapter III, "The value of a strategic plan", framing investment opportunities in the context of the firm's plan allowed leadership to reach consensus more rapidly on lateral and group acquisitions that in the past might have required more lengthy internal deliberation. As Proskauer chair Tim Mungovan explains:

> *We're executing on the strategic plan and making our decisions around laterals. We've pushed forward on some laterals in terms of speed of execution in ways that are new for us. When chief competitor X is bidding up a candidate that we really need, we have looked at each other and said, "Is it in the plan? Okay, we're going to give it a little extra juice here," and we have given it a little extra juice that is different in ways and in terms than we have done in the past.*

For example, the firm has prioritised investment in partners and teams who grow and complement the firm's market leadership in private credit, including in structured products.

> **Takeaway:** Building out a nimble hiring process is rooted in a clear strategy and disciplined execution. As is usually the case, this is just as important as having and following a plan.

Most firms outside the top 15 by profits per equity partner are actively considering M&A, and even within the top 15, some are beginning to ask questions about M&A and whether it should be on the table for their firm going forward.

VI. Strategic M&A: accelerating the plan

1. Introduction

The strategic imperative faced by most firms – to rapidly and simultaneously grow their size, profitability and market leadership – is leading to more focus on M&A. Firm leaders increasingly feel that M&A should at least be on the table alongside other alternatives, given accelerating segmentation, the risks of not growing size and profitability enough relative to competitors, and the reality that, net of retirements and departures, growing with laterals alone is usually slow, error-prone and expensive.

A key driver of segmentation is compensation paid to partners. Available benchmarking about partner compensation confirms that larger and more profitable firms within a given competitive set pay their partners more, starting at the top among the highest-compensated partners, but also often among lower-compensated partners too.

The extent to which this advantages larger and more profitable firms relative to peers has grown sharply in recent years due to compounding elements that have driven wider differentials between firms. Put another way, many firms that compete directly with larger and more profitable firms have had a steep hill to climb to attract and retain strategically important partners and teams. This is an important

Figure 1: Compensation – all partners (CAP) growth in Am Law 100 segments

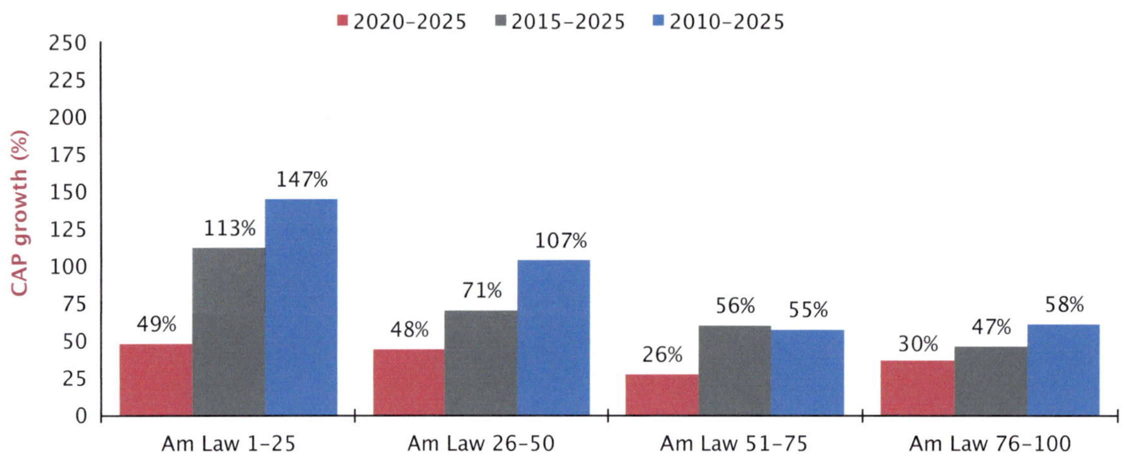

reality that underpins the growing interest in M&A, including among many already large and high-performing firms.

While high-profile mergers have long occurred in the marketplace, in recent years the size, profitability and brand strength of firms interested in transactions have evolved considerably. More high-performing national and international firms, with widely respected brands in their chosen areas of focus, have put M&A on the table to accelerate progress in highly desirable practices, sectors and cities that would advance the achievement of their strategy. Most firms outside the top 15 by profits per equity partner are actively considering M&A, and even within the top 15, some are beginning to ask questions about M&A and whether it should be on the table for their firm going forward. Some firms are going through an exercise of holding a mirror up to themselves, thinking about how they would look to hypothetical future merger partners, and quietly taking steps to get themselves ready to be as attractive as possible.

Wall Street firm Shearman & Sterling was in the top 10 Am Law rankings not more than 25 years ago. The firm, embattled by partner departures and slumping size and profitability relative to its peers, announced a merger with British firm Allen & Overy in 2023. The combination created a new $3.7 billion entity, A&O Shearman.

Kramer Levin was also a New York-based firm with a strong legacy reputation that had started to fall behind its peers in size and profitability, and therefore in flexibility on compensation. Soon after the departure of a key partner to Gibson, Dunn & Crutcher, a much larger and more profitable firm, and facing the threat of additional regrettable departures that could have unravelled the firm, Kramer merged with Herbert Smith Freehills to create Herbert Smith Freehills Kramer, a

Figure 2: Am Law 200 revenue per lawyer (RPL) increase 2000–2025

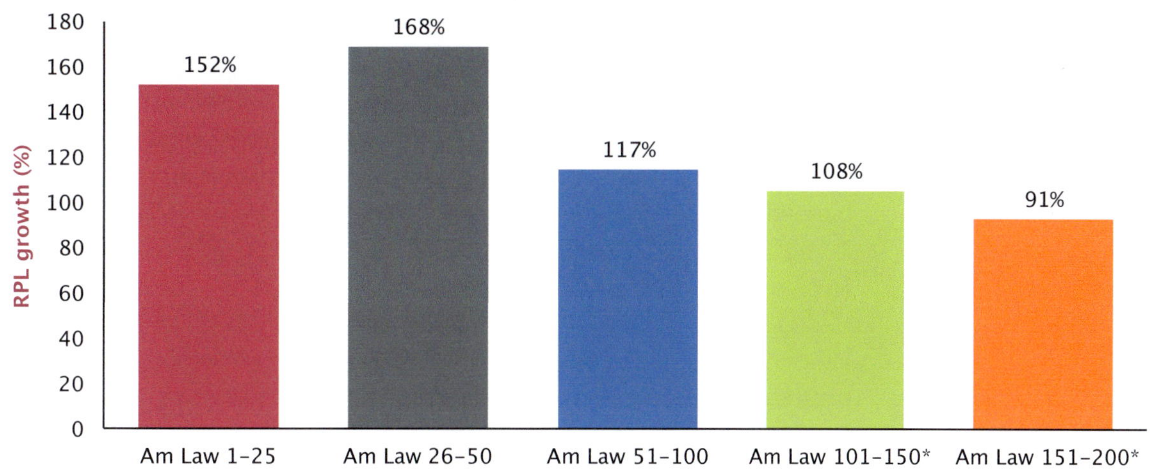

* Am Law 101-150 and 151-200 represent 2000-2024 growth rates due to lack of publicly available FY25 data for the second hundred.

multinational $2.7 billion entity. More recently, Schulte Roth & Zabel experienced a series of departures of practice group leaders and others to larger and more profitable firms, and then combined with a larger firm, McDermott Will & Emery.

The impact of scale has been so profound in some money centres, such as New York, that firms with annual revenue between $300 million and $1 billion have found it difficult to keep up with their larger and better-resourced competitors. As such, they have become prospective merger partners for larger firms.

In this chapter, we examine how two recent law firm mergers came together and assess the firms' motivations. We will hear from Ira Coleman, chairman of the newly merged McDermott Will & Schulte, and Mitch Zuklie, chairman and CEO of Orrick, Herrington & Sutcliffe, which combined with Buckley in 2023, as they candidly discuss how they steered their partnerships to consider and successfully consummate a merger.

2. Global platform meets New York

The 2025 merger of McDermott Will & Emery and Schulte Roth & Zabel exemplifies the combination of a large, international firm and a smaller, money-centre firm.

McDermott Will & Emery, founded in 1934, built its reputation by being a leader in areas such as tax, healthcare, private client and transactions. In the 1990s, with shifting market conditions and strong business developers, the firm extended its historic strength in healthcare to gain traction at the intersection of private equity and healthcare. McDermott later expanded its reach in the private equity space by carving out a niche at the intersection of private equity and other sectors, including insurance and energy.

Schulte Roth & Zabel, by contrast, had a fifty-plus-year history of serving private capital-focused clients. Formed in 1969 by three partners who left traditional Big Law practices, the New York-based firm's trajectory tracked the ascent of alternative asset classes, handling transactional work and litigation for a wide range of players in the private asset world, from hedge funds and private equity funds to distressed-debt buyers and others.

While Schulte was highly profitable relative to most firms of its size – profits per equity partner were north of $4 million in 2024, according to Am Law data[1] – it was nevertheless a relatively small firm in the highly competitive New York market, competing against many larger and more profitable firms to serve private capital-focused clients. Put another way, Schulte ranked in the bottom 10% of Am Law 100 firms by gross revenue, and much larger competitors had come to dwarf Schulte in some of the very practice areas that the firm had once pioneered in New York. The impetus for a merger was less about the firm's internal dynamics and more about the shifting competitive landscape, as larger, more profitable firms benefited from compounding scale and began to pull away with a considerable talent advantage.

McDermott's growth strategy led to its interest in a transformative merger, although it was not always on the hunt for a specific partner with a specific specialty, according to chair Ira Coleman.

At the firm's annual retreat of its executive committee, Coleman, like the leaders of many firms, regularly discussed with his partners the best available alternatives to grow and to achieve the firm's aspirations:

> *We've always had a growth mindset. We put the consideration on the table and made a list of firms. We were very diligent and took a pragmatic approach – looking at various opportunities through a consultant lens. We had initial conversations, but at the end of the day, even though those firms are great, we saw that most opportunities hit a natural roadblock and wouldn't pan out. I think the training for the Schulte merger and our ability to execute on it quickly was through prior merger attempts. It was going down the path with others that gave us insight into what we needed to prioritize.*

The success of some smaller acquisitions positioned McDermott to know what to expect in pursuing and combining with another firm. McDermott, for example, had acquired and integrated new tax and intellectual property practices in previous decades. For this reason,

Coleman advises other firm leaders to consider even small mergers to understand the virtues and challenges of incorporating another firm into the mix:

> *It doesn't have to be big. What I recommend is doing a little one first. I think it's good to stretch the muscles – it's law firm chair 101. Let's say you're a very cautious football coach who rarely calls onside kicks. That's fine, but you should still practice them. Over time, this practice creates the muscle memory needed for when the real opportunity arises. And when it does, your odds of success are exponentially higher.*

Coleman believes that merger talks often turn on questions of management and governance, and while firms often say publicly that they strive for an equal combination of the two firms, exact parity is not always beneficial to a new entity. Creating a shared management structure that is top-heavy is not optimal for a merged firm, says Coleman: "This is really the best advice I could give people: more lawyers running a law firm is not good." If both firms have 20 people on their management committees, he points out, building a combined committee of 40 people will not be helpful:

> *The way lawyers think about these things is really interesting, but it's not business-focused. Instead, the focus should be on finding the best way to run the integration to make sure that the combined firm is protected.*

To Coleman, that in part means getting buy-in and acceptance from the new partners:

> *The sooner I could treat you like one of my partners in every single way for every single reason, and the more authority you vest in us to run the firm, a collective firm, the more successful and better off we're going to be.*

McDermott and Schulte publicly announced they were in merger talks in May 2025 and swiftly finalised details, officially merging in August of that year. The newly combined McDermott Will & Schulte took in close to $3 billion ($2.9 billion) in annual revenue in 2025 according to Am Law, putting it in the Am Law 10 band of firms by gross revenue.

More importantly, the firm is now positioned to compete in areas that its legacy parts did not have the scale and depth to compete as successfully in; and those possibilities, explains Coleman, are motivating for the partners of the combined firm:

"Everyone is energised to chase an aspirational peer group – a group that we weren't even talking about or involved with a year ago ..."

Ira Coleman, chair, McDermott Will & Schulte

> *A law firm chair might say: "Why take this risk?" But, I think the rewards can be amazing, and that's what we're seeing. Everyone is energised to chase an aspirational peer group – a group that we weren't even talking about or involved with a year ago – and now we are. There's always room to aim higher, even at the top, and this is an extraordinary catalyst.*

Coleman uses a football analogy to describe the ambitions of the combined firm:

> *We covered the ball and now we're going to drive down and score the touchdown. And it's energizing.*

Nevertheless, he says, executing on those ambitions is in the early stages:

> *Make no bones about it – the hard work is to come.*

Looking back, Coleman offers advice to other law firm chairs who may be considering merging or acquiring another firm. The driving force of a merger, he says, should be the desire for the two firms to win collectively:

A firm should never merge with or acquire another firm simply to enhance its own practice ... I'm not a fan of thinking that a strategic merger should only be beneficial to you. In fact, it's got to be better for them than for you. And then, if you're lucky, everything goes right, and the investments pay off, you will come out with a stronger, unified firm. The rewards are tangible: better growth with your big clients and greater momentum in the strategic areas you've identified as being important.

Coleman has this warning, however:

Deal fever can be tempting, but if people aren't going to do better on the collective platform, don't do the merger. Good lawyers will leave and you'll be stuck with the bad apples who don't have better options and will poison the well for everybody.

Takeaway: Retaining key partners of both firms and mitigating the risk of regrettable departures during or after a merger often requires creating a platform and position that is more valuable to them than other platforms on which they could practice.

3. A culture of improvement

In 2023, Orrick merged with Buckley, a boutique firm based in Washington DC that specialises in financial services regulatory and enforcement matters.[2] This merger was motivated by a clear recognition of specific strategic gaps within Orrick that, if addressed, could strengthen its position and enhance important client relationships. By serving clients across more practices in areas that Orrick has prioritised for growth, the firm aims to deepen these relationships.

Additionally, Orrick's culture of innovation played a significant role in the decision to pursue and successfully finalise this strategic combination. Orrick, with its roots in the San Francisco Bay Area, had developed a sector-focused approach – refined over time – to build market leadership in technology and life sciences, energy and infrastructure, and finance.

The firm saw a tremendous opportunity to strengthen its offering for clients focused on the intersection of technology and finance. Both firms saw a market trend – technology clients were quickly becoming financial services companies at the same time that traditional financial services clients were becoming technology companies. Although it had a long-time Washington DC practice, the firm had set a priority to build out its financial regulatory practice, including to support its strong and fast-growing portfolio of fintech clients.

[I]f an acquisition or a merger can accelerate progress towards a market position a firm is already striving to reach, leaders of many high-performing firms are increasingly evaluating the advantages and disadvantages of a transaction (or more than one) to get there alongside the advantages and disadvantages of growing organically and with laterals alone.

Orrick chair Mitch Zuklie explains:

> *There are certain areas of intersection that we are focused on growing because we have an inherent competitive advantage relative to others. We had good finance lawyers, technology lawyers, litigators, dispute resolution lawyers, transactional lawyers. We are good at fintech financings, IPOs and M&A deals, but we were not so good at fintech regulatory and enforcement. We had a hole there.*

And the firm predicted that the need for regulatory and enforcement work would only grow for its clients, at the federal or state level, or both.

Zuklie's approach – viewing a potential merger as an accelerator to build more dominant and well-rounded market leadership in areas of focus by extending existing areas of strength – is a strategy that often distinguishes how high-performing firms frame their thinking about the possibility of an acquisition or merger.

Put another way, if an acquisition or a merger can accelerate progress towards a market position a firm is already striving to reach, leaders of many high-performing firms are increasingly evaluating the advantages and disadvantages of a transaction (or more than one) to get there alongside the advantages and disadvantages of growing organically and with laterals alone.

Meanwhile, Buckley's singular focus was on financial services regulatory and fintech work, but, he says, the firm "wanted more depth to be able to cover clients' full life cycle".

Orrick's culture of commitment to constant improvement led to a willingness to identify strategic gaps and to learn from the laterals it attracted. That was foundational to the firm's successful merger with Buckley, Zuklie explains:

> *There's this culture around embracing change, innovation, learning from people with new ideas, and challenging ourselves. Part of our culture is to embrace critique, take it seriously and think about the things we can change and improve on in order to be increasingly relevant, more inclusive, less bureaucratic, and to deliver greater value to our clients. This is another way laterals make us stronger – and we ask every one of them what we can learn from their prior experience.*

Orrick conducted a cost–benefit analysis to evaluate whether a merger was the best path, looking at other options short of a transaction. This approach – particularly considering all available alternatives to achieve a firm's strategy, including the alternative of not transacting – is common among the leaders of high-performing firms. Buckley made a similar assessment about becoming a part of a larger firm. Zuklie recalls:

> *We had to think: is it sufficiently important on the regulatory and enforcement side for us to make such a large investment in this particular vertical of 100 lawyers? There's a lot to integrate and a lot of time, attention, energy. Are we better off hiring 20 lawyers in the market rather than bringing in a whole firm? Both sides had to evaluate it. And we both thought it was more valuable, particularly at a moment when innovators and traditional financial services leaders were navigating greater regulatory uncertainty at the federal and state level.*

With more than 1,000 lawyers in offices around the world, Orrick dwarfed Buckley, given Buckley had about 100 attorneys and five offices in Washington DC, New York, Chicago, Santa Monica and San Francisco. Nevertheless, Buckley's premium position in fintech regulatory work and the value to Orrick of filling that hole prompted Orrick to view the combination as something other than a big firm acquiring a smaller one. As Zuklie says:

Alignment on common cultural attributes is often as important as, or more important than, strategic alignment between the firms. As management consultants often say, culture eats strategy for breakfast. That is particularly true in law firm mergers.

> *One of our guiding principles when we did the Buckley transaction was to treat our new team like it was a complete merger, not an acquisition, even though we were a much larger organisation. [This was accomplished] by having them share pieces of their culture that would make us better, of which there are many. ... They were doing service delivery differently than we were. They were more nimble than us. They helped us streamline our approach to doing things. We were made much stronger as a firm from many of the ways they operated.*

One aspect of Buckley's approach to service delivery that was appealing to Orrick was Buckley's drive for technological innovation. Buckley had created a vast database of state and federal financial services laws, which it had monetised in the form of various custom products for clients.

Looking back nearly three years after the merger was finalised, Zuklie notes that the integration, while substantial, was nevertheless a better fit than attempting to attract dozens of comparable laterals:

> *It's for sure the case that it is more efficient than ones and twos. Imagine the efforts of identifying, strategizing, interviewing so many laterals. And further, it's a team that came in with a strong culture of collaborating and with a leadership that have become absolutely integral to our leadership.*
>
> *The bottom line is I think we were made much stronger as a firm by the many ways they operated as a firm and by their cultural norms. Three years later, I think both sides would agree it turned out, in most ways, to be even more valuable than expected.*

Zuklie again chalks up the success to culture and willingness:

> *There are certain cultures that are more inclined to benefit from M&A than others.*

Takeaway: Alignment on common cultural attributes is often as important as, or more important than, strategic alignment between the firms. As management consultants often say, culture eats strategy for breakfast. That is particularly true in law firm mergers.

Notes

1 *The American Lawyer*, 2025 Am Law 100 rankings, available at www.law.com/americanlawyer/am-law-100/.

2 The new, combined firm retained the name Orrick, Herrington & Sutcliffe.

VII. Accelerating strategic growth

1. Introduction

The rise of new asset classes in the financial markets, particularly the significant growth of private equity and, more recently, private credit, has led to substantial changes in the market for legal services. These changes include the emergence of market-leading firms in certain areas, and a dramatic increase in hourly rates. Additionally, there has been the formation of new practice groups and increasingly aggressive competition for specialised talent, fuelled by the substantial resources accumulated by firms that have experienced significant growth and profitability over the past decade. As a result, some firms have adapted and evolved to remain competitive in this changing environment, while others have struggled to keep pace.

In this chapter, we look at how three firms in different segments of the market have demonstrated new paradigms to develop high-performing practices in particularly competitive areas. Each firm represents a different approach.

One firm, Proskauer Rose, led most of the market in building a leading practice focused on a growing, specialty asset class – private credit. Another, McDermott Will & Schulte, built a formidable practice at the intersection of a long-time sector strength, healthcare, and private equity. The third, Davis Polk, built a leading practice at the intersection of its historic transactional strengths and new asset classes.

We will hear from the leaders of each of these firms about how they successfully competed to develop a position of market leadership in crowded areas inundated with intense competition.

2. Riding the private credit wave

Tim Mungovan, the chair of Proskauer, likens his firm's choice to invest in serving the private credit market to a very different pastime than practising law. To Mungovan, it was like surfing:

> *Our partners saw the wave. They're on the board, in the ocean, and they saw the wave coming, and they said, "We're going to get on this wave." And they made a choice. You have to pick the right wave. You have to pick which one you would get on. Picking the right wave is one thing; riding it is another; you have to match the speed of the wave; get up on the board; then you have to own the wave, getting others to back off, and concede the territory so that you have control.*

Proskauer's tale of ascendancy in this space is one of grit, perseverance and hard work. It grew a one-time niche practice and

"You have to pick which one you would get on. Picking the right wave is one thing; riding it is another; you have to match the speed of the wave; get up on the board; then you have to own the wave..."

Tim Mungovan, chair, Proskauer Rose

became a dominant player that is now competing head-to-head with a growing group of very high-performing rivals also competing in the private credit space.

Private credit, commonly known as privately negotiated debt financing provided by non-bank lenders directly to businesses, expanded following the 2008 recession: global assets under management were about $500 billion in 2014 and are projected to reach about $3 trillion by 2028, according to a 2025 Moody's report.[1]

Mungovan compared Proskauer's experience in private credit to other firms that have had real success in particular markets and have outperformed, such as Kirkland & Ellis in private equity. Mungovan traced Proskauer's role in the space, like Kirkland's, to the very inception of the asset class. The firm's early days in the practice, which goes back more than 20 years, came into focus when partners Stephen Boyko and Steve Ellis,[2] both with significant lending practices, simply had, according to Mungovan, a Rolodex of names that they were going to call. "I think that they were just scrappier," he said. "Our people hustled."

The practice was originally known as junior capital, and later as mezzanine finance, and when the industry began branding itself as private credit, Proskauer's lawyers gained momentum. Mungovan explains:

> *They did an excellent job of branding themselves and going out and seeing every player in that space and just pursuing every deal, doing as many deals as they could for as many as many clients as they could. I would say that they've institutionalized the practice over the last six or seven years and really transitioned it more broadly to other lawyers.*

Mungovan names several of the firm's leaders in particular: Gary Creem, the group's first associate hire and now a co-head of the private credit group; Sandra Montgomery in Los Angeles; and Michael Mezzacappa and Justin Breen in New York.

But Mungovan is aware that while an early mover has an advantage, it cannot stand still: competition from larger players has grown as the asset class has taken off and continues to grow. As we noted in Chapter II, "The benefits of competitive scale and profitability", firms that have achieved greater scale relative to their rivals typically have more resources to recruit and retain talent, and are often seen as a safer choice by both sought-after talent and clients for sophisticated matters.

Aware of the evolving competitive landscape and dynamics, Proskauer's leadership team developed a strategic plan to sustain its differentiating strengths in private credit as more firms compete in that space as it matures. Mungovan says:

> *We are in what I'll call the middle stages of riding that wave where, in some ways, we really have to double down and make further investments with the expectation that the ride is going to continue. Like everything at a middle stage, the competition from other firms is flooding into the market because they're seeing the opportunity. We are a prime target because we were early, and we have a lot of talent that has been through the market's build-up. We have done a good job of retaining our talent, but we need to continue to invest in our key practices to maintain our competitive position.*

Armed with a consensus-driven strategic plan – see Chapter III, "The value of a strategic plan" – Mungovan and his partners increasingly invest in areas adjacent to their private credit practice. The firm's plan prioritises expanding these practices while also expanding into related areas, such as private equity transactions and M&A. As Mungovan explains:

> *What I try to say to people is: the best market to be in is in an expanding market where you're a market leader, because you're going to be able to grow at least at the rate of the market, and probably at a faster rate than the market if you're a market leader.*

Takeaway: Dominant market leadership in an area of growing demand where clients will pay premium rates is a tried-and-true path taken by firms that outperform their peers, leading to outsized growth of revenue and profits.

3. Pioneering a new model

The success of many rising outperformers lies in an engine the firms have developed at the intersection of a rapidly growing sector and a rapidly growing asset class. In McDermott's case, the sector is healthcare, and the asset class is private equity.

Ira Coleman, McDermott's long-time chair, encapsulates the firm's strategy as "marrying great skill sets to a great vertical. That's how you get one plus one equals three."

The successful strategy dates to the 1990s, when McDermott began scaling up a practice in the rapidly changing healthcare industry. The efforts began with Larry Gerber, a McDermott partner who served as the firm's chair from 1991 to 2003. As Coleman explains:

> *We became the first firm to have a dedicated health law practice, even before Larry took over as chair. It started with us doing reorganizations for various not-for-profit companies, healthcare companies, and hospital systems. It was a creative way to get value and give back healthcare services.*

At the time, the industry was undergoing rapid change, as consolidation and acquisitions by for-profit enterprises were transforming prevailing business models. "We just kept moving upmarket, and we always led with education," says Coleman.

Education, as Coleman describes it, became a key aspect of McDermott's business development strategy. The firm began by hosting no-frills conferences to educate industry leaders about market trends and attract their business. "We didn't even have PowerPoint yet," recalls Coleman. "We had little slides that were made on a slide carousel." The conferences centred on the latest trend: hospitals buying physician practice groups.

> *This was back in the mid-90s. It was a flourishing industry and we were at the forefront. We were teaching the health systems about it. We understood the tax implications and where the biggest challenges and opportunities were.*

As the healthcare sector grew, so too did McDermott. It took on laterals and groups, growing the firm's offices in Chicago, Boston, Washington and Miami, and expanding its transactional expertise as well as regulatory practices such as antitrust and FDA compliance.

> *[That experience] solidified two things for us. One is, you've got to grow. And two is, if you follow an industry and that's what you want to do, you better be the best in the industry. You have to develop it.*

The firm assembled a deep and formidable healthcare practice, handling corporate work for hospitals, building expertise in FDA and regulatory matters and intellectual property work. The firm won Health Care Team of the Year from Chambers in 2010 and has received the award several times since.

Chambers routinely names McDermott a Band One firm for its healthcare practice. The healthcare play laid the foundation for a much bigger expansion: marrying its healthcare practice with a private equity practice. As Coleman explains:

> *The key is anticipating what's next and being on the forefront of that. When I came into the story, we were seeing a major shift in healthcare: ownership was moving away from governments,*

municipalities and religious organizations to private investors. Once a hospital was no longer owned by these traditional groups, consolidation was the next inevitable step, which translated into transactions. Investors didn't want a single hospital – that model doesn't work for business. They wanted 10 hospitals so they could capture economies of scale. It just made sense.

He adds:

So, we were in on the ground floor of this, and again, we led with education. I'd say, around 18 years ago we said, "Hey, let's find out what private equity thinks about this."

Once again, the firm's business development and education efforts were central to its entry into private equity's expansion in healthcare. "We invited private equity leaders who were investing in healthcare to Miami for a conference to talk about this shift," explains Coleman.

The first conference was not exactly a blockbuster affair, but fast forward to present day, and Coleman says the firm's Miami healthcare private equity conference now regularly draws about 2,000 attendees. This and other conferences and events draw many thousands of attendees today.

The result has been a robust practice that advises a broad portfolio of private equity sponsors and health-related companies on transactions.

McDermott has distinguished itself from many healthcare-focused rivals by achieving a highly competitive level of profitability and scale, including a global presence with 24 offices worldwide. And in August 2025 McDermott's ambitions to further accelerate its growth were sealed when it closed its merger with Schulte Roth & Zabel. Am Law data reveals that the new combined firm took in $2.99 billion in 2025, creating a new Top 20 law firm in the Am Law 100.[3]

The success in merging the healthcare practice with a private equity practice, says Coleman, has led the firm to replicate its success in other sectors:

Once we were able to prove the concept in healthcare, we did it in other verticals. We have a big alcohol, food and beverage practice. We have an energy practice, both traditional and renewable, which are two separate functions. And our newest one is insurance tech.

The overall approach of giving more than we get, however, has always been part of our culture, whether it's education, connections or community.

[U]sing a 'halo' that a firm earns in the minds of clients for going deep into a sector can help it get traction in highly competitive areas like PE and M&A.

Coleman goes on to explain how the firm's investment in many signature events, trade groups, and other business development efforts has translated into valuable new relationships and work:

> *We helped found the Healthcare Private Equity Association, which we're the General Counsel of, and we continue to grow and develop. We used that as a tip of the spear to get into a bunch of private equity firms doing non-healthcare work. Once a client experiences our team, they come back – whether the next deal is in data centers, energy, or something else entirely. So, we've used our healthcare expertise as a model to expand across the private equity landscape.*

Takeaway: As McDermott's experience demonstrates, using a 'halo' that a firm earns in the minds of clients for going deep into a sector can help it get traction in highly competitive areas like PE and M&A. The power of the halo grows at the intersection of high-demand areas and high-rate markets. This approach helps firms entering newer areas become more credible market leaders, whether in competitive practices such as PE or in challenging markets such as New York.

The shifts in corporate dealmaking and the rise of private money in more and more headline-making and middle-market and larger transactions have spurred some firms with traditional corporate transactional practices – that long relied on investment banks and blue-chip clients – to seek change.

4. Tradition meets change

Firms that developed and operationalised long-term strategies tied to 'money practices' – such as those that target sophisticated transactions involving private equity and other alternative asset classes involving private money – have become dominant players in the corporate league tables in the last 10 years, with firms such as Kirkland & Ellis, Latham & Watkins and Paul Weiss regularly rising and sometimes topping league table deal charts.

The shifts in corporate dealmaking and the rise of private money in more and more headline-making and middle-market and larger transactions have spurred some firms with traditional corporate transactional practices – that long relied on investment banks and blue-chip clients – to seek change. Some firms have adapted more successfully to the change than others.

One firm that accelerated its plans for change, given the competitive environment, is Davis Polk. The firm had a traditional practice representing underwriters in capital markets work and blue-chip companies in M&A transactions.

Its profits-per-partner rankings were always high. Yet midway through the last decade, the firm observed the frenzied deal pace and volume of significant private equity transactions and realised it needed to expand its practice to capture the heightened dealmaking of private equity firms and their sponsors.

"In 2015 to 2016," says Davis Polk chairman Neil Barr, "we really began to focus on private equity M&A in a way that we had not historically. And we've been very, very successful in that."

At that time, it became clear that the traditions of Wall Street client relationships were undergoing changes that would have a significant impact on the life cycle of a corporate client for a traditional corporate firm like Davis Polk and the way it is selected to handle corporate deals – a trend that Brad Karp of Paul Weiss alluded to in Chapter IV, "Compensation as strategic accelerator".

As Barr explains:

> *The way that underwriters now hire lawyers is different from the way it was 20 years ago. It's not like you just pick up a phone and call Davis Polk and the banks have favors to repay in the same way. And if you had an issuer client, you got a corporate client, and a corporate client produces M&A, and it produces litigation and other types of work. The thinking about the return on investment of these efforts and where it goes over a period of time has been part of the analysis as well.*

"In 2015 to 2016, we really began to focus on private equity M&A in a way that we had not historically. And we've been very, very successful in that."

Neil Barr, chair, Davis Polk

Amidst all of this disruptive change, Barr says, the firm saw a need to grow its M&A and private equity work along with other complementary areas:

> *As we did that, it became clear that we needed the synergy within the private fund formation business. And the same has been true with some of the credit businesses as well. I think if you woke my partners up in the middle of the night after a couple of annual meetings and said, "Where do we have holes? What do you think?", they would say private credit.*

The result, notes Barr, is that over the last several years, the firm has reimagined its central pillars, adding asset management as a major piece of the firm, in addition to practices that "have been in the Davis Polk history book forever", such as capital markets, M&A, finance, restructuring and litigation.

The push into additional asset classes has been bolstered by several lateral hires – a relatively new frontier for Davis Polk. In addition to taking on a group of fund formation partners from Debevoise & Plimpton in August 2024, in March 2025 the firm lured Michael Diz, a Debevoise partner with deep ties to the private equity industry who has long handled work for TPG and Providence Equity Partners. In

2022, Davis Polk also brought in Paul Scrivano, a deal lawyer then at Ropes & Gray with a deep practice in both public and private company M&A.

The firm regularly handles work for TPG and Crestview Partners and, in 2025, advised Sycamore Partners on the acquisition of Walgreens Boots Alliance, which was valued at around $10 billion.

As Barr notes, the firm is incredibly tactical about its hiring and practice choices: some of the firm's practices, such as financial regulatory or IP work, "we don't want to scale in the same way we want to scale the other ones". Nonetheless, he says, these practices all represent "the connective tissue that ties Davis Polk as a firm together".

Takeaway: Traditional Wall Street firms and other rising competitors around the country have broken out of some of their older moulds and adapted to prioritising at the intersection of their historic strengths and newer asset classes. This, and aligning their approach to compensation with accelerating the achievement of their strategy, has improved their financial performance and market position. Other firms have been slower to adapt, and some have regressed in size and financial performance relative to today's outperformers.

Notes

1 Moody's 2025 Private Credit Outlook, www.moodys.com/web/en/us/insights/buy-side/three-key-trends-shaping-the-future-of-asset-management.html.

2 Steve Ellis chaired Proskauer from 2020 to 2024, preceding Tim Mungovan.

3 See also, McDermott Will & Schulte press release, "Top law firms finalize merger, debut McDermott Will & Schulte as new legal powerhouse", 4 August 2025, /www.mcdermottlaw.com/media/mcdermott-will-schulte-new-legal-powerhouse/ .

VIII. Leading through change

1. Introduction

From their very beginnings, most law firms have been partnership-driven institutions, built on consensus, in which culture is important.

To grow, evolve and make choices that lead to a sustainable competitive advantage, outperforming firms increasingly rely on effective and proactive leadership. Many of these successful firms have leaders – either one or a few individuals – who hold significant credibility within the partnership, enabling them to make important decisions that benefit the firm's overall interests. Effective leaders recognise that they cannot please every partner with every decision; therefore, they focus on addressing the interests of the high performers in their firm and nurturing the next generation of talent, especially those who are crucial to the firm's success and the most valuable to retain. Brian Fahrney, chair of Sidley Austin's executive committee, explains:

> *Law firms just behave much differently than they did 10 or 15 years ago, and I think that's only accelerating. If firms are going through change and the industry is going through change, leadership has to be credible to make sure that a firm is able to make the hard decisions to navigate through those changes. As leaders, we have to make sure we have the support of the firm, the key partners, and the clients to do that.*

Yet it can be challenging for law firms to find enough effective leaders to navigate these dynamics. Often, the partners who rise to the top of their practice – and are in line to take over the leadership of their firm – do not have prior experience leading a large organisation.

In addition, the currency of credibility in law firms generally comes from being seen as an excellent lawyer and excellent business developer, not necessarily from the perception of excellence as a CEO type. That said, outperforming firms tend to have people with the credibility to lead and the attributes required to be excellent, effective leaders. Fahrney observes:

> *There is a common denominator for good leaders. At least at one point in their career, they were respected practitioners. They were generating business, and they were viewed that way internally by their firm. I think that in order to become an effective leader, you have to have credibility. You have to have the history of having been a strong revenue generator and a strong practicing lawyer because you are trying to manage a large group of lawyers who are also are good at those things.*

In this chapter, we analyse how various firms have managed change, identify the characteristics of effective leaders in high-performing

[T]he currency of credibility in law firms generally comes from being seen as an excellent lawyer and excellent business developer, not necessarily from the perception of excellence as a CEO type.

firms and investigate how these firms have transitioned leadership from one generation to the next.

2. Aligning management and governance with strategy

Outperforming law firms often have a common experience when it comes to leadership: they tend to align their approach to management and governance with what it takes to accelerate the achievement of the firm's strategy.

At Sidley, the firm's management and governance approach features two leaders effectively serving as co-chairs: Brian Fahrney and Yvette Ostolaza. The firm has a larger leadership body called the 'executive committee', comprising around 40 partners and chaired by Fahrney. Additionally, there is a smaller group known as the 'management committee', consisting of nine partners. This committee is a subset of the executive committee and is chaired by Ostolaza. While there are numerous effective approaches to management and governance, many firms tend to adopt an approach and structure similar to Sidley's as they grow in size and complexity. Fahrney notes:

> *Large law firms have become a lot more complicated. There are a lot more moving pieces. People are moving in, people are moving out. Attracting and retaining talent is huge, and the talent is more mobile, and the job is bigger. Having two people with the credibility of saying they are a chair of a firm can just help you get more done. There are some real benefits to having two heads available. Think of whatever the task du jour is and you have different strengths. You have different time commitments and availability. One of us is always going to be available. I think, particularly on some of the tougher things, you're going to come to better decision making with two chairs.*

Fahrney's co-chair Yvette Ostolaza echoes the point:

> *We're really working day-in, day-out together. It's not often that we get a call that one of us doesn't know about. Two is better than one. I think our structure is a great balance. We're running a global operation. We have each other's backs and we're being consistent.*

Importantly, as Ostolaza notes, this approach to management allows for a range of voices to be heard by Sidley's leadership as the firm grows and ascends. With approximately 2,300 lawyers, the firm has more than 20 offices worldwide. Committee members are an even mix of career-long Sidley partners and laterals, representing a range of career experiences and perspectives on strategic growth, financial performance, culture and market leadership. According to Ostolaza:

Streamlined management informed by diverse perspectives can lead to more efficient consensus-building and better management decisions.

> *Because of our executive committee, our representative body, the power does not lie in one place. It's dispersed. I think it's important not to live in an echo chamber.*

At Sidley, the management committee oversees compensation – a common approach, says Ostolaza:

> *I really believe that in professional services organizations, the people on the business or management committee must have the compensation function. And at our firm, at least in its current iteration of the committee, it's a very powerful, business-oriented committee that has the respect of the partnership.*

Takeaway: Streamlined management informed by diverse perspectives can lead to more efficient consensus-building and better management decisions.

3. Small firm, big presence

Firms don't have to be large to choose to have co-leaders at the top.

At Wachtell, Lipton, Rosen & Katz, culture, strategic priorities and size inform the firm's approach to management and governance. Wachtell is led by co-chairs Andrew Nussbaum and Bill Savitt, who assumed the role in late 2023 and represent the firm's culture.

"We have to be a place where you know every partner," says Nussbaum.

Most law firm partners relinquish most or all of their practice when they become their firm's leader; the job is simply too demanding to pair with a full-time practice in most outperforming firms. However, Savitt and Nussbaum have not given up their practices.

Nussbaum is a partner who specialises in M&A and private equity. He has successfully completed a series of headline-making cross-border and other transactions involving mergers between US and European companies. He advised OpenAI on a $6.6 billion funding round in October 2024 that increased its valuation to $157 billion,[1] and subsequently on the recapitalisation of OpenAI into a public benefit corporation at a valuation of $500 billion.[2]

Savitt is a trial lawyer known for his significant role in high-stakes corporate governance and mergers and acquisitions litigation in the Delaware Court of Chancery and other courts across the country. Notably, he represented Twitter in its lawsuit to enforce Elon Musk's purchase of the company.

Nussbaum and Savitt are fully dedicated to their practices, continuing the legacy of their predecessors, Daniel Neff and Edward Herlihy, as well as the founders, Martin Lipton and Herbert Wachtell. As Nussbaum explains:

> *This is a place where the partners are actively engaged in leading the matters. While Bill and I are happy to help manage the firm forward, neither of us would want it as a full-time job.*

Wachtell's management team includes two of the firm's most senior partners: one from corporate and the other from litigation. Although Wachtell is primarily recognised for its success in public company transactional work, its litigation practice has helped create a more balanced approach. This balance allows the firm to integrate both cyclically driven and acyclical practices, which is increasingly common among top-performing firms. By achieving this balance, firms can maintain more consistent performance through varying economic cycles and provide their clients with broader and more reliable services across different practice areas.

According to Savitt:

> *It was new to have a litigation partner in an executive function. I think it's very much appreciated by the litigation group. The corporate group is the largest group in the firm, and it's not close,*

> *but the litigation group is the second largest group. I've been the co-chair of the litigation department for over 10 years, and in that time I think we have improved the department. We've become much better at justifying and charging premium fees in the litigation context.*

But, says Savitt, the firm's reputation as a juggernaut in the M&A world was not always the same as its reputation in the world of high-stakes litigation, at least not initially:

> *Premium billing in the litigation context is not easy, and it's harder than in M&A. We've had a lot of wins over the course of 10 years in high-profile matters that have allowed us to increase the public profile and the client- facing reputation of the group. We're still an M&A firm, first and foremost, I think, and much of where we're most successful litigating is in the context of either merger and acquisition disputes or corporate governance-type problems.*

In this way, Wachtell is extending its existing strengths in building newer, highly competitive areas for the firm. This is common: outperforming firms often gain traction in highly competitive practices and cities by extending their existing strengths to differentiate themselves and compete successfully against other firms.

Savitt says the firm's work has garnered the attention it was hoping for in the market:

> *[W]e are now competitive across the board, in commercial litigation and trial work in a way that I think wasn't the case 10 years ago. And that has been reflected in the profitability and the internal prestige of the department.*

4. Deference to leadership

In contrast to Sidley and Wachtell's approach to firmwide co-leaders, Kirkland & Ellis has a sole firmwide leader, chair Jon Ballis.

"You have to break down the walls," explains Ballis. "You have to break the structure in order to scale, but redo things in a way for the new world."

Kirkland's management structure affords Ballis considerable deference, a key factor in the firm's ability to grow and evolve rapidly. Successfully recruiting needle-moving laterals and groups, crafting competitive compensation packages and making hard choices to strengthen the firm are decisions that do not require large committee debate and approvals at Kirkland. In fact, these decisions can be made in hours, not weeks, says Ballis:

Of course, if we're going to do something material, I call key people, key constituents and stakeholders, and make sure that they're on board, or at least close enough on board.

But even the firm's management committee, he says, rarely takes a vote at meetings. This is something Kirkland has in common with many high-performing firms. As Ballis says:

We don't operate that way. It's a very CEO sort of structure. You might say it is the classic benevolent dictatorship. My job is to aggregate information 24 hours a day so that when the decisions come, it puts me in the best position to get it right.

Takeaway: Outperforming firms are increasingly adapting their culture and approach to management and governance to be somewhat less democratic and more deferential to leadership in making important decisions, thereby leaving it to leadership to determine the degree of consensus-building necessary, depending on the decision. As part of this shift, some firms have amended their partnership agreements to make it easier for the leader or smaller leadership groups to approve the admission of new equity partners or the counselling out of partners who underperform expectations for years without a good reason.

[O]utperforming firms often gain traction in highly competitive practices and cities by extending their existing strengths to differentiate themselves and compete successfully against other firms.

Leaders of firms that outperform typically lead the seemingly insurmountable task of protecting the best of their firm's culture while accelerating growth in firm size, profitability, quality and market leadership in chosen areas.

5. Leading with culture

Leaders of firms that outperform typically lead the seemingly insurmountable task of protecting the best of their firm's culture while accelerating growth in firm size, profitability, quality and market leadership in chosen areas. This requires managing competing priorities and striking a balance that advances the firm's vision and goals. "How do you maintain the culture in a vast network?" remarks Ballis. "That's hard, and to be honest, it's why I travel a ton. It requires you to get your hands dirty."

Kirkland has long been known as a firm that values business generation, tenacity and attention to client service – qualities that are fitting for a firm historically built around serving a base of growing private equity clients, clients in the midst of high-stakes litigation and businesses going through transformative bankruptcies and restructurings.

For Ballis, what amounts to retail politics more or less – going to the firm's many offices, communicating with people directly, in small groups, through firmwide bulletins – is a means to driving cohesion, protecting the best of the firm's culture while also driving constant improvement:

> *I'm like, this is my job. I walk around, talk to people, listen – and again, I'm not trying to pretend like I have some secret sauce or something like that. It's me. It's just sort of like doing your job.*

On many trips to Kirkland's far-flung offices, Ballis wanders the floors where associates are sitting and introduces himself, asking questions like, "What are you guys working on? What schools did you go to? What do you like? What things can we do better?"

He believes in maintaining connections:

> *Sometimes we have these little interim town halls. It takes a massive amount of effort, not just for me, but from everyone in the network. During COVID, we started this weekly email to keep people connected. And I kept it going, and I'm raw and honest, quite transparent about it.*

This regular, multi-channel communication and candour seems to resonate within the firm:

> *I'm like, "You know, last month was a disappointment. We thought we were going to do better." Or "You know, this particular business was really good. This one was soft." I send it to the whole firm, secretaries, staff, the highest partners. You have to be intentional and proactive to keep the culture in a wide network.*

Ballis, who was originally a lateral to Kirkland from Sidley and rose in the firm as a deal lawyer handling multibillion-dollar deals on behalf of private equity clients, represents one model of law firm management, acting as something akin to a CEO of a public company. Ballis no longer practices law and spends his days on chairman duties full-time, travelling to Riyadh and New York and dozens of other cities while overseeing day-to-day decisions and interacting with important clients.

Ostolaza, of Sidley, similarly notes that she and Fahrney regularly communicate the firm's multifaceted strategies and priorities across its global operations when they speak at firm events:

> *We haven't said, "There's one strategy." This is a big operation. There's enough for everybody. There's a regulatory strategy, there's a bankruptcy strategy, there's a European strategy, and we're sensitive to that. We go out of our way in every presentation that we do, every speech, every event that we are covering, to say we are the global operation that we are.*

Takeaway: It is an increasingly common practice among firms that outperform to align their management and governance approaches with the requirement to accelerate the execution of strategy. In a growing group of firms that outperform, this means an approach that is less democratic and more akin to a benevolent dictatorship, with targeted consensus-building when material decisions are being made.

6. Grappling with succession

One of the toughest choices firms face in shaping their future is selecting who will lead the firm next.

Finding someone with the attributes to lead a firm successfully is not always easy. And the attributes required to effectively lead may be different from one firm to another, depending on culture, market position, the aspirations the partners have and what it will take to achieve them.

Successful firms prioritise individuals with credibility who excel as both lawyers and business developers. Key qualities include strong financial acumen, emotional intelligence, good listening skills, and the ability to navigate difficult conversations and make difficult decisions. These individuals chart a course for their firm's future with their firm's best interests in mind; effectively recruit and retain high-value talent; counsel others out who are undercutting the firm's performance or culture; build consensus among diverse stakeholders; enhance the firm's visibility with journalists; and nurture important client relationships.

Successful firms prioritise individuals with credibility who excel as both lawyers and business developers. Key qualities include strong financial acumen, emotional intelligence, good listening skills, and the ability to navigate difficult conversations.

To succeed in most top-performing firms, individuals need to be prepared to relinquish most or all of their legal practice to take on leadership roles. Once in these positions, many firmwide leaders find the job to be quite challenging. This difficulty arises because law firms typically operate as flat organisations filled with intelligent and accomplished individuals. Most of these individuals are trained to identify issues and are naturally sceptical, often believing they know every question and answer.

For all of these reasons, most law firms do not have an oversupply of people who have the credibility to lead and who are willing and able to be excellent, effective firmwide leaders.

Step one in the leadership succession process is the prevailing view that power must be passed to younger leaders. While some firms have term limits or retirement ages, what's paramount is that firm leaders are cognisant of the need to cede power, notes Ostolaza. "I love what I do," she says, "but we should leave room for the next generation, always."

Like many firms, Sidley's process centres on staggering the terms of its two co-chairs and allowing a relatively long lead time for selecting and grooming the next leaders. Fahrney explains:

You don't have two new faces, you have one at a time. People can get accustomed to the new co-chair while still having the familiarity of the existing one – it's less disruptive that way.

Firms that excel at leadership transitions address the transition with ample lead time, often starting years in advance, with a year (sometimes more) for the new person to be involved in a full cycle of compensation, budgeting, year-end collections, promotions and rate increases. "A theme of good transitions," says Fahrney, "is just coming to consensus in a non-adversarial way."

Sidley's process is for a well-respected member of the firm's management committee to be identified by the other members (including the outgoing chair) and gradually groomed as a successor.

In addition to this approach, some firms engage specific partners, while others leverage outside advisers to interview a sample of both formal and informal leaders on an unattributed basis. These interviews focus on identifying the attributes that the next leader will need to possess to be successful in the role, and which partners have those attributes, in addition to having the credibility to lead the firm successfully.

In some firms, the leadership team then divides up the rest of the partners and conducts similar unattributed interviews with every partner in the firm. When this is done, some firms wisely segment the input to know the views of the high performers versus the views of medium and low performers.

Takeaway: Leadership transitions often serve as critical turning points for organisations. Firms that excel during transitions typically have a well-established process that allows for ample lead time and is trusted by the partnership. Some firms may ask the outgoing leader to select their successor, while others strive to reach a consensus on the essential qualities the next leader should possess. They then identify partners who have not just these attributes, but also the credibility to effectively lead.

Notes

1 See Shirin Ghaffary, Katie Roof, Rachel Metz and Dina Bass, "OpenAI Raises $6.6 Billion in Funds at $157 Billon Value", Bloomberg, www.bloomberg.com/news/articles/2024-10-02/openai-has-closed-new-funding-round-raising-over-6-5-billion.

2 See Reuters, "Microsoft and OpenAI reach new deal valuing OpenAI at $500 billion", available on the NBC News website at: www.nbcnews.com/tech/tech-news/microsoft-openai-reach-new-deal-valuing-openai-500-billion-rcna240255.

IX. The rise of the business professional

1. Introduction

Outperforming firms have distinguished themselves by bringing their operations in line with mainstream businesses, particularly high-performing, larger firms that have resources to invest in top-tier C-suite talent. One way they do this is by investing in highly impactful business leaders and other professionals and adding effective functional support in areas such as finance, technology, knowledge management, data analytics, marketing and business development, and other functional areas.

While law firms have long relied on business professionals to run some aspects of their business, including certain mid- and back-office functions, some outperforming firms have taken these professional positions to the next level. They are hiring and retaining influential C-suite-level leaders who oversee armies of professionals, some of whom are far more influential and sought-after today than in years past.

These firms are not turning over the reins to business professionals; rather, they are leveraging professionals whose core competencies lie in running an increasingly complex business more effectively and competitively, on par with leading professional service firms and other sophisticated businesses. Firms that have achieved a high level of growth and profitability have the resources and flexibility to make large investments in managing and running their operations. Available benchmarking data we have collected indicates that large and more profitable firms pay C-suite leaders far more than smaller and less profitable firms.

For example, Simpson Thacher & Bartlett has hired several professionals from consulting firm McKinsey, including Liz Grennan, the firm's chief client officer, and Suraj Sharma, its chief knowledge and innovation officer. In June 2025, Kirkland & Ellis hired a new COO, Gary Levin, whose experience included a senior role at private equity giant Blackstone Group, a client of the firm. Levin oversees Kirkland's 3,000-plus staff of administrators and business professionals. Ropes & Gray has several executives who had previous experience at Boston Consulting Group.

In this chapter, we look at the journeys of C-suite executives at two firms – Latham & Watkins and Sullivan & Cromwell – to explore the value that deeply experienced, high-level business leaders regularly contribute to outperforming firms. The trend, of course, is not limited to these two firms: many of the highest-performing firms have made significant investments in needle-moving business professionals. The result is that these firms often have more firepower to take on big challenges and opportunities.

Firms that have achieved a high level of growth and profitability have the resources and flexibility to make large investments in managing and running their operations.

2. The beginnings

Karen Braun, executive director of Sullivan & Cromwell, and LeeAnn Black, chief operating officer of Latham & Watkins, have unique but different perspectives on the rise of the business professional in law firms; they have both witnessed and participated in this evolution. Their personal stories illustrate the importance of this role to their firms' success.

"The role has gone from reactive to proactive strategic leader," Braun notes.

Braun's own journey maps this change. She worked for more than 13 years at Kirkland & Ellis, rising to chief marketing officer, where she worked closely with the firm's management, principally on strategic marketing and business development efforts that coincided with Kirkland's rise to dominant market leadership in private equity, public M&A, products liability litigation, restructuring and other areas.

In 2009, she joined Sullivan & Cromwell, where she rose to become the firm's executive director. She now oversees the business side of a firm with approximately 1,000 lawyers across 13 offices in major financial centres worldwide.

LeeAnn Black rose through the ranks from the financial side, a common path for many top COOs in outperforming law firms. After beginning her career as an auditor at Arthur Andersen, Black joined Latham in the late 1980s. "I joined Latham in a financial role when the firm had $300 million in revenue," she recalls.

In the early 1990s, Latham was virtually unknown in New York, where Black was based. After Black rose to the COO role in the late 1990s, she began working closely with then-chairman Robert Dell, a transformative leader in the firm's rise. Dell had joined Latham in 1982 after the firm acquired Hedlund, Hunter & Lynch, where he was practising, and went on to serve as the firm's chair from 1994 to 2014. Under Dell's leadership, the firm grew by more than 1,500 lawyers, dramatically grew its profitability, and expanded its reach nationally and internationally, opening new offices across the United States, Europe, Asia and the Middle East.

Black has been instrumental in Latham's historic rise to become one of the largest and most profitable law firms in the world. Latham reported $8.3 billion in gross revenue in 2025. As Black recalls:

> *From the beginning I was deeply involved in firm strategy. I was on the project with McKinsey that looked at [the question of] do we go global, or do we not? It sounds kind of silly today, but at the time*

that was a huge open question, and we had to build consensus around whether to do it at all.

Takeaway: The role of outstanding business professionals might have had somewhat humble beginnings, but it has evolved considerably in the last 10 years. Today, very few outperforming firms lack a COO or equivalent position held by a highly qualified business professional who oversees the firm's operations and is increasingly involved in executing the firm's strategy.

3. Importance of C-suite role

C-suite professionals – COOs, chief marketing and business development officers, chief technology officers, chief talent officers and others – play critical roles at high-performing firms. A number of firms, particularly larger and more profitable ones, have elevated their most senior business professionals to leadership positions that work hand in glove with the firm's most senior equity partners.

The top tier of these professionals oversee a staff of hundreds or thousands of administrative and business professionals. Their oversight includes building out and managing the firm's finance function, talent recruiting and development, pricing, marketing and business development, technology and AI, strategic use of research and data, real estate and facilities, and more.

In many cases, these C-suite executives even weigh in and are often influential on matters such as rate-setting, lateral partner hiring and decisions to de-equitise and counsel partners out of the firm. Increasingly, COOs and certain other C-level leaders not only have a seat at the management table but are also strong influencers and, in some cases, joint decision makers on board-level decisions.

As with the war for talent for lateral partners, firms are increasingly competing for top C-suite talent. These trends point to another reason firms with greater scale and profitability are well positioned for the future: they can invest in seasoned business leaders who are indispensable to enhancing their performance and position.

It is critically important, says Black, that there is an open and ongoing dialogue between C-suite professionals and the firm's executive committee:

It sounds simple, but these individuals [our C-suite leaders] and their teams are responsible for executing on the executive committee's strategy, and the executive committee is relying on their subject matter expertise to make sure we think through all of the issues and ultimately get it right.

As with the war for talent for lateral partners, firms are increasingly competing for top C-suite talent.

C-suite leaders who demonstrate their strengths and contributions to the firm's executive committee or management committee can gain their trust and help the firm by constructively contributing to significant decision making. Black comments:

> *Trust takes time to earn, but ultimately our firm is a meritocracy and I have seen a number of senior [administrative] professionals become indispensable to our business over the years.*

Black epitomises the model of a business professional deeply involved in overseeing the firm's financial performance. Many regard her as someone who runs the firm day-to-day, although she does not describe herself that way:

> *The partnership agreement gives broad authority to the executive committee, which is made up of some of our busiest and most successful partners. You need a robust team of dedicated professionals behind them to get things done to execute on firm strategy and priorities – financial experts, business development professionals, technologists and many others. I'm proud of the role that our team plays in that regard.*

Black also regularly interviews potential lateral partners and is involved in most significant decisions the firm makes, including, for example, office openings, real estate strategy and technology investments. She is also a driving force behind the ongoing evolution of Latham's internal and client service offerings.

Black has helped bring many new professional roles and services online throughout her tenure and has expanded the business services staff to include well-being experts, partner integration resources, economists, data scientists, machine learning engineers, physical security experts, architects and many other roles that previously did not exist in the law firm setting.

At Sullivan & Cromwell, Braun works closely with key leaders to oversee significant firm-wide initiatives, a common aspect of C-suite leadership. She describes a recent initiative where S&C was looking to replace the firm's outdated document management system:

> *It was a bespoke system housing decades of information – in fact, I believe more files than The Library of Congress. Knowing we needed to change, we created a group that included: S&C leadership, partners proficient in global data privacy issues and intellectual property, practice and office managing partners, technical and information security experts, and various department heads within S&C to study our options. We determined cloud-based technology, with significantly stronger encryption, was a better long-term solution than an on-premise system, which was the industry standard.*

Braun explains that when the project began at the end of 2020, no other Am Law 20 firm had made a similar migration to the cloud. In fact, some client guidelines specifically stated firms could not use cloud-based applications with their data.

> *We identified clients with these rules and met with them, discussing why we thought the cloud-based approach could be in everyone's best interest. Realizing that some clients were financial institutions bound by regulatory compliance issues, we met with former regulators, explaining our strategy with this new system.*

The project also faced challenges from the outbreak of the global COVID-19 pandemic, which had just started in early 2020. The virus brought the world to an abrupt halt, with the majority of people working remotely. S&C pivoted, holding the majority of its meetings, demonstrations and trainings on Zoom. "Fast forward to today," says Braun:

> *Our document management system has been a huge success,*

allowing our lawyers and business professionals the ability to create, save and find documents, whether at their computer or on mobile devices, much more quickly compared to our old system, saving time for our lawyers and ultimately our clients. Designing a ground-breaking approach for the move of documents to the cloud gave us the know-how to develop a strategic approach for AI.

That team was assembled because of Braun's access to S&C's leadership and the confidence they placed in her ability to get the job done. "This demonstrates," she says, "the differences in the COO or executive director role from yesterday to today: from a doer to a member of the strategic team."

Takeaway: The scope of work performed by COOs and other C-suite leaders has grown in the last 10 years, and firms with more scale and profitability have had greater flexibility to invest in highly impactful leaders who can become among the most valuable people in their firms.

4. Leadership traits

Playing a leadership role as a business professional in a legal partnership is, of course, not always easy. Both Braun and Black have risen to the upper echelons of their firms through determination and hard work – and thanks to other traits that they say are crucial to their success. To be successful and help drive a firm's success, Braun explains, C-suite professionals benefit from having a deep and nuanced appreciation for the complex and specialised work that law firms do:

I need to understand all the transactional and litigation issues in order to be able to work collaboratively with my partners. When people try to break into the legal profession, some do not have the vernacular to be able to communicate effectively on a variety of legal and business subject matters, and it undermines their credibility with lawyers, business professionals and clients of the firm.

Braun explains that when she works alongside S&C partners, "The partners focus on the significant economic, legal and partnership issues. My role is to consider the business issues and work with a broad team to make ideas come to life."

LeeAnn Black points out that a successful C-suite leader has the dual ability to help maintain aspects of a firm's culture – in Latham's case, its transparency – while driving and overseeing its financial performance. Black's combination of credibility, financial acumen and transparency has helped her direct and manage the firm's finances, strategic vision and vast operations:

> *It's important to have confidence, empathy and humility when asking hard questions and making hard decisions. I've found that giving partners context for why decisions are made and insight into the process goes a long way to generating consensus and buy-in, even when they don't necessarily agree with the outcome.*

5. Long reach

Another driver of success is a COO's ability to have a 'long reach', which Black describes as the ability to both oversee and drill down on a variety of topics, including technology/AI, information and data analytics, marketing and public relations, finance, operations, human resources, legal recruiting and professional development, all while knowing what clients they serve and how.

A recent example of Braun's far-reaching initiatives is the implementation of AI within the firm. As of early 2026, thousands of legal software companies purport to save time and money through the use of AI. Braun says:

> *I have seen AI presentations on the legal side from transactions to litigation management, and on the business side from business development to process improvement. I question if we aren't seeing an AI bubble similar to the dotcom bubble, where only the strongest companies will survive. But AI success really is about strong*

As of early 2026, thousands of legal software companies purport to save time and money through the use of AI.

leadership. It is in the implementation, training and long-term development of the system – otherwise it is vast amounts of information floating without a captain.

Professional leaders, particularly those who have expertise in finance, talent management and technology, have a unique window into the future of the business of law. A select group of leaders at forward-looking firms – often firms that have the internal resources to invest in future-looking initiatives – are indeed looking to the future, and in particular to the dual promise and threat of generative AI. Black explains Latham's approach:

As always, we're focused on adding resources that will be critical to the future of our business, and in the tech space we've hired up over time, adding new roles such as cyber security professionals and data scientists. When it comes to our AI strategy, we've got a dedicated AI team with senior leadership both on the legal side and the technical side. On the front lines, we have what we call innovation lawyers who are working side-by-side with our practicing lawyers, and also with our machine learning engineers, to figure out ways in which we can use AI and other new technologies to streamline workflow and enhance client service.

Black goes on to explain that Latham's AI strategy is both technology-driven and people-centric:

We were one of the first firms to implement a way to use ChatGPT within our firewall so we can leverage it in a manner that maintains confidentiality and security. People are now using it in their daily workflow and it's highly effective in both our client service and our business operations. We are also focused on customizing third-party products that are highly effective, but ultimately the most important thing is training and adoption – you need the best lawyers using the best technology. That's what maintains your position as a market leader and allows you to strengthen your competitive advantage – we're fortunate to have a culture that is rooted in innovation and embracing change, and the result is excitement and enthusiasm for the opportunities that AI provides for client service and internal operations.

Based on survey data, only a small number of firms anticipate making leverage or staffing changes in response to generative AI capabilities in the next two years. But a significantly larger proportion of firms say they expect AI to facilitate those changes by 2034.

Firms do recognise the disruptive power of the technology, but most see it as manifesting in full several years down the road.

While drivers of success in the current market emphasise competitive size, profitability, investment resources, quality and market leadership in chosen areas, other major changes are also coming down the pike.

Conclusion

We were inspired to write *The Outperformers: Lessons from Top Law Firm Leaders* to share one of the most fascinating parts of our work: candid conversations with leaders of firms that consistently outperform the market – and with leaders of firms that are actively ascending in that direction.

While some of the elements discussed are specific to Big Law firms, many of the market forces and other topics we explore apply to any firm in a competitive market, large or small, on a relative basis.

Many of these successful firms achieved their success by proactively making strategic choices to address changes in market dynamics – particularly the growth of new asset classes, increasingly fierce competition to retain and attract talent, and evolving cultures across many firms. In other words, many high-performing firms were able to make hard choices and change what needed to be changed to meet the aspirations of their high-performing partners.

While drivers of success in the current market emphasise competitive size, profitability, investment resources, quality and market leadership in chosen areas, other major changes are also coming down the pike, and the firms profiled here will need to continue evolving to adjust to those as well.

This report did not focus on artificial intelligence, for example. While every major firm is exploring its uses, as of this writing, AI is not a significant driver for outperformance among the firms on which we focused. But that seems certain to change – it would be hard to find a firm leader or attorney who didn't believe that AI will significantly alter the legal landscape in ways both known and unknown in the coming years.

As some firms have found – for various reasons outlined in this report – the ability to adapt in meaningful ways to changing conditions is paramount not just to surviving but to thriving.

[T]he ability to adapt in meaningful ways to changing conditions is paramount not just to surviving but to thriving.

About the authors

Kent Zimmermann
Zeughauser Group
zimmermann@consultzg.com

Kent Zimmermann is widely regarded as one of the leading strategic advisers to law firm leaders in the United States and beyond. For more than two decades, he has advised many of the world's most high-performing law firms on firm-wide strategy and strategic combinations. Working with his partners and team of associates and analysts, he has advised 10 of the 20 most profitable US law firms and more than 80% of the Am Law 100.

Kent is particularly known for his work on complex, high-stakes law firm mergers and other strategic growth initiatives. He served as a principal adviser on the largest law firm mergers announced in 2024 and 2025, including the largest in history.

He co-authored *Law Firm Mergers: Lessons from Successful Strategic Combinations*, published by Globe Law and Business in 2022. He speaks and publishes frequently, and is a Law.com Fellow. He lives in Newport Coast, California.